PRAYING
WITH
SAINT
BENEDICT

REFLECTIONS
ON THE RULE

Praying with Saint Benedict

Reflections on the Rule

STEPHEN ISAACSON

Morehouse Publishing
NEW YORK

St. Benedict's Rule for Monasteries is translated from the Latin by Leonard J. Doyle. Copyright 1948 by Order of Saint Benedict. Published by Liturgical Press, Collegeville, Minnesota. All rights reserved. Used with permission.

The Scripture quotations contained herein are from the New Revised Standard Version Bible, copyright © 1989 by the Division of Christian Education of the National Council of Churches of Christ in the U.S.A. Used by permission. All rights reserved.

Morehouse Publishing, 19 East 34th Street, New York, NY 10016
Morehouse Publishing is an imprint of Church Publishing Incorporated.

Cover design by Marc Whitaker, MTWdesign
Typeset by Rose Design

Library of Congress Cataloging-in-Publication Data

Names: Isaacson, Stephen, author.
Title: Praying with Saint Benedict : reflections on The rule / Stephen Isaacson.
Description: New York : Morehouse Publishing, [2021]
Identifiers: LCCN 2021018032 (print) | LCCN 2021018033 (ebook) | ISBN 9781640654464 (paperback) | ISBN 9781640654471 (epub)
Subjects: LCSH: Benedict, Saint, Abbot of Monte Cassino. Regula. | Devotional literature.
Classification: LCC BX3004.Z5 I83 2021 (print) | LCC BX3004.Z5 (ebook) | DDC 255/.106--dc23

LC record available at https://lccn.loc.gov/2021018032
LC ebook record available at https://lccn.loc.gov/2021018033

CONTENTS

PREFACE

"HAVE YOU EVER ANSWERED GOD'S CALL?" she asked, in her characteristically direct manner. My friend Jo, spiritual director, lay leader, and restless Methodist, had just related her reasons for leaving one job and taking another and was curious to know whether God spoke to me in similar ways. Had I ever answered God's call? I responded that, yes, I think I had.

More than ten years ago, I sat in a Wednesday evening catechesis class, in part to support my partner who wanted to take the class, and in part to probe my interest in taking my faith more seriously. The guest speaker, Elaine Harris, spoke about intentional communities and, in particular, Cornerstone, a Benedictine community of about thirty-five people within Trinity Episcopal Cathedral's congregation in Portland, Oregon. She talked about their practice of the Rule of Benedict and the things they valued, such as restraint of speech, following a rule of life, and prayer. She ended by leading the class in a Compline service from the Book of Common Prayer. As she spoke, I thought about my desire for friends with whom I could pray and talk about my spiritual life. I was so profoundly moved by Elaine's words and my response to them that I rode home in silence, unable to say anything to my partner at the wheel for fear that my voice would break. I thought about it for days afterward.

I had to wait several months before taking the weekly class on Benedictine spirituality that was offered the next fall. During the first class session, I couldn't help but wonder why any monastic group—even a lay monastic group—would want me as a member. I had never had an interest in saints or things monastic. I didn't then have a regular prayer practice. I felt like a spiritual midget. And yet, the following January, I stood in front of my Cornerstone brothers and sisters with a lump in my throat and pledged stability, obedience, and conversion of life.

Rachel Held Evans wrote that what is most annoying and beautiful about the Holy Spirit is that it has this habit of showing up in all the wrong places and among all the wrong people.[1]

So began my life in a Benedictine community. With my Cornerstone brothers and sisters, we study the Rule of Benedict and, in small groups, try to apply it to our day-to-day lives. We read and discuss Benedictine authors

---

1. Rachel Held Evans, *Searching for Sunday* (Nashville, TN: Nelson Books, 2015), 197.

such as Thomas Merton, Esther de Waal, Cynthia Bourgeault, Michael Casey, and—of course—Joan Chittister. Being part of this community has been transformational for me.

About two years ago, wanting to spend more time in the Rule, I adopted a Lenten project of writing personal reflections on each of the chapters in the Rule. I had the same challenges every twenty-first-century person has with a guidebook written in the sixth century. It was of a certain time and place, written long before the study of psychology or progressive theology, and in some respects seemed very severe according to today's standards. However, within the Rule, looking past the culturally specific distractions, were appealing guidelines for living in community: the practice of deference to each other, the importance of prayer throughout the day, the value of the Psalms in worship, the necessity for humility and restraint of speech, the gift of hospitality, and always the need to maintain a balance between discipline and charity.

When I was first introduced to the Rule of Benedict, I had one lurking misgiving. In my strict evangelical upbringing, I was taught that scripture was the authoritative source for knowing how to live our faith. Where does the Rule fit in? Shouldn't I be looking to the Bible, rather than to the Rule, for answers regarding how I should live my life?

I was calmed by these two discoveries as I read the Rule: First, Benedict himself makes frequent reference to scripture throughout the text. In nearly every chapter he cites short passages from the Gospels, the Psalms, and the Epistles. Clearly, scripture was his source for knowledge on the practice of faith and living in community, as it has been for other Christian writers. Second, Benedict points, in his final chapter, to Christ and to the "divinely inspired books of the Old and New Testaments." He goes on to recommend other religious texts from leaders of the early church. He modestly describes his Rule as a *minimum* guideline written for beginners.

One of my intentions, then, in writing my personal reflections was to explore the scriptures that Benedict cites in his short chapters in their full context. I discovered that words and phrases were different in Benedict's translation of the Bible from the ones we tend to use today. Sometimes he lifts quotations out of their original context, implying somewhat different meanings than the biblical authors originally intended. In the chapters where he does not quote scripture, I have looked for scripture that I think applies to the principle he is expounding. Each of the chapters in this book, therefore, includes at least one scripture passage that sheds light on Benedict's teaching.

Each chapter begins with a passage from the Rule, using the Doyle translation. The passage from the Rule is followed by a scripture passage, using the New Revised Standard Version.

Lectio divina is an ancient practice of prayerfully reading scripture. It is personal reflection during which, through repeated reading, we try to inwardly digest the substance of the passage, believing God speaks to us through the sacred text.[2] Although there are several recommended formats for engaging in *lectio divina*, Columba Stewart states that it is really a disposition more than a method.[3] It is meant to be a conversation with God about one's life. It is with that intent that I have included three contemplation questions after the two readings to draw you more deeply into the texts.

Then follows the reflection. In keeping with its intended use as devotional reading, I also have ended each chapter with a prayer.

---

2. Mariano Magrassi, *Praying the Bible* (Collegeville, MN: Liturgical Press, 1998), 18ff.

3. Columba Stewart, *Prayer and Community: The Benedictine Tradition* (Maryknoll, NY: Orbis, 1998), 39, 41.

ACKNOWLEDGMENTS

ELAINE STEWART HARRIS INTRODUCED ME TO the Rule of Benedict, Benedictine practice, and the Cornerstone community at Trinity Episcopal Cathedral in Portland, Oregon. She has been my spiritual exemplar and mentor ever since, and I am very grateful for her loving leadership and spiritual encouragement as abbot of our lay community.

I also give thanks for members of the Cornerstone community and particularly to the individuals I meet with weekly who read early portions of this work and gave me encouraging feedback, especially Ron Walker, my brother in Christ, who not only responded with enthusiastic encouragement but gave me the very good idea of including *lectio divina* questions as part of each devotional reflection. Being witness to his spiritual journey has been an inspiration to my own.

I have to thank Amelia De Vaal who, having experience in the world of publishing, offered to read the first draft of the book, gave me valuable feedback, and encouraged me to find a publisher. My friend of many years, Margaret Benefiel, connected me with Church Publishing. Thanks are owed to Nancy Bryan, my editor, for her gracious and positive communication and for suggesting a different structure for the book.

My brother, Jim, has always understood that I needed to take a different spiritual path than his own, and I give thanks for him and his family who have never shown me anything but wholehearted love. I also have had the joy of living with Michael Pickrell, the most loving person I have ever known, for over twenty-five years now. He has encouraged and supported me in every effort I've undertaken.

INTRODUCTION

BENEDICT AND THE RULE

Benedict of Nursia was born in 480 CE, the son of nobility. Long before Italy had been united as a country, Nursia (or Norcia) was part of the Umbrian district of Perugia, governed by Rome. As a young man, Benedict was sent by his parents to Rome to study but became disgusted by the decadence that he witnessed there, even among the clergy, and the political influence of the rich and powerful on the papacy. He left his studies, retired to the Simbruinian hills, and later became a hermit, living in a cave beside a lake above the town of Subiaco.

However, in spite of his isolation, he must have had social contact with other individuals, who then sought him out for advice and spiritual guidance as the fame of his sanctity spread. The local bishop asked him to form a community of the various monks in the area and become their abbot. Like many others who have stepped into a leadership position for the first time, his efforts were not completely successful. In fact, legend has it he was so unpopular with the monks in his first monastery that they tried to poison him. The legend also says he was saved by a raven who swooped down and stole a piece of poisoned bread out of Benedict's hand before he could eat it. The raven is now a standard image in many icons of Saint Benedict.

However, Benedict went on to found twelve monasteries, including Monte Cassino, the largest (now a popular pilgrimage destination), where he wrote his Rule for Monasteries (540 CE). There is no evidence that he intended to found a monastic order, but in the early ninth century Louis the Pious declared that the Rule of Benedict would be the blueprint of organization for all monastic communities. The Order of Saint Benedict that evolved is one of the earliest and arguably the most influential. To put his influence in perspective, it is interesting to note that Benedict produced his Rule in the first part of the sixth century, while the Franciscans and Dominicans were established in the thirteenth century, the Jesuits in the sixteenth century, and the Cistercians and Trappists in the seventeenth century.

Benedict's Rule borrowed from other sources, most notably from the writings of John Cassian and an existing rule by an anonymous "Master," which gave a more authoritarian role to the abbot. Among the challenges for modern readers is the fact that Benedict wrote his rule for monks (that is, males), and today it reads as very male-centric, ignoring the fact that there are thousands of women monastics as well. Translations do exist that have attempted inclusive language, the most successful being Joan Chittister's.[1] The Order of Saint Benedict website uses a version of Leonard Doyle's translation that somewhat awkwardly attempts inclusive language by the use of "Abbot" and male pronouns in one chapter, and "Prioress" and female pronouns in the next, alternating this pattern throughout the text. I have chosen instead to use the original translation by Doyle,[2] while acknowledging that there are thousands of women Benedictines who follow Benedict's Rule. I ask their indulgence, appreciating the context and times in which the Rule was written.

Benedict's more gentle and balanced guidelines for leadership and discipline may, in fact, be due to a feminine influence in his life. He was very close to his twin sister, Scholastica, who consecrated her life to God at an early age. She founded and governed a monastery of nuns, about five miles from Monte Cassino, and Benedict became her superior. They visited each other once a year, spending their time in prayer and conversation on spiritual matters.

Benedict wrote the Rule as a modest "little rule for beginners." Its popularity and its power lie in its practicality, clear and direct text, and balance—between discipline and forgiveness, between authority and mutual support. Its influence has survived the Reformation, dissolution of the English monasteries, and various revolutions. It has strongly informed the Anglican liturgy and the Book of Common Prayer. Today it remains a guide for almost nine thousand Benedictine monastics worldwide as well as countless lay followers who find in it inspired wisdom as they pursue their spiritual journey in the secular world.

---

1. Joan Chittister, *The Rule of Benedict: Insights for the Ages* (New York: Crossroad, 1992).

2. Benedict of Nursia, *St. Benedict's Rule for Monasteries*, trans. Leonard J. Doyle (St. Louis: B. Herder Book Co., 1935). Project Gutenberg, 2015. http://www.gutenberg.org/files/50040/50040-h/50040-h.htm.

1

RESPONDING TO GOD'S CALL

LISTENING

From the Rule

Listen, my son, to your master's precepts, and incline the ear of your heart. Receive willingly and carry out effectively your loving father's advice, that by the labor of obedience you may return to Him from whom you had departed by the sloth of disobedience.

To you, therefore, my words are now addressed, whoever you may be, who are renouncing your own will to do battle under the Lord Christ, the true King, and are taking up the strong, bright weapons of obedience.

And first of all, whatever good work you begin to do, beg of Him with most earnest prayer to perfect it, that He who has now deigned to count us among His sons may not at any time be grieved by our evil deeds. For we must always so serve Him with the good things He has given us, that He will never as an angry Father disinherit His children, nor ever as a dread Lord, provoked by our evil actions, deliver us to everlasting punishment as wicked servants who would not follow Him to glory. (Prologue, Part 1)

Proverbs 4

10 Hear, my child, and accept my words,
   that the years of your life may be many.
11 I have taught you the way of wisdom;
   I have led you in the paths of uprightness.
12 When you walk, your step will not be hampered;
   and if you run, you will not stumble.
13 Keep hold of instruction, do not let go;
   guard her, for she is your life . . .
20 My child, be attentive to my words;
   incline your ear to my sayings.

[21] Let them not escape from your sight;
keep them within your heart.

Contemplation

1. What word, phrase, or image from either of the two passages resonates with you?
2. What connection can you make to your own life?
3. What might God be calling you to do?

Reflection

The Prologue to the Rule of Benedict concisely presents all the key themes that are elaborated upon throughout the rest of the Rule. Many have noted that Benedict starts, in the very first sentence, with the injunction to *listen* and highlights the importance of eager, responsive listening, or listening "with the ear of your heart." So, it is not only important that my ears are open, but that my heart is open as well.

Benedict immediately introduces the subject of obedience (not my favorite spiritual topic). One might question Benedict's theology here, anthropomorphically making God an angry parent who, enraged by our sins, threatens to disinherit us. But Benedict correctly knows that the one who loves us (God) wants to bring us back into right relationship with God, back from our slothful indifference. It is not coincidental that the topics of listening and obedience are linked here. The Latin word for obey, *oboedire*, can also mean "to listen to." And, of course, for those of us who willfully want to control our own lives, obedience will also require a spiritual transformation, a conversion of life.

Prayer

Loving and merciful God, forgive me for the times I disregard your will in my life. Open the ears of my heart to listen to your instruction, open my eyes to see your love all around me, and direct my steps in obedience to your Word. Amen.

WAKING UP

From the Rule

Let us arise, then, at last, for the Scripture stirs us up, saying, "Now is the hour for us to rise from sleep" (Rom. 13:11). Let us open our eyes to the deifying light, let us hear with attentive ears the warning which the divine voice cries daily to us, "Today if you hear His voice, harden not your hearts" (Ps. 95:8). And again, "He who has ears to hear, let him hear what the Spirit says to the churches" (Rev. 2:7). And what does He say? "Come, my children, listen to Me; I will teach you the fear of the Lord." (Ps. 34:11). "Run while you have the light of life, lest the darkness of death overtake you" (John 12:35). (Prologue, Part 2)

Romans 13

[11] Besides this, you know what time it is, how it is now the moment for you to wake from sleep. For salvation is nearer to us now than when we became believers; [12] the night is far gone, the day is near. Let us then lay aside the works of darkness and put on the armor of light; [13] let us live honorably as in the day, not in reveling and drunkenness, not in debauchery and licentiousness, not in quarreling and jealousy. [14] Instead, put on the Lord Jesus Christ, and make no provision for the flesh, to gratify its desires.

Contemplation

1. What word, phrase, or image from either of the two passages resonates with you?
2. What connection can you make to your own life?
3. What might God be calling you to do?

Reflection

"Rise and shine, it's quarter to nine!" my dad used to call up the stairs every Sunday morning, signaling it was time to get up, get dressed, and get ready for church. Benedict is saying something similar to us: Get up, wake up, listen, and "run while you have the light of life." His tone is urgent.

Many of us come to a point in our lives when, because of having aged, or suffered through a life-threatening disease, or experienced the death of a loved one, we are keenly aware that we have only a certain number of days to become the person that we want—and God wants us—to be. We may have been sleep-walking through much of our life or coasting along in our faith. It's time to wake up.

Benedict is echoing the Holy Spirit's call: Come, listen, learn to reverence God. Put on the Lord Jesus Christ. There is work for us to do in the kingdom of heaven.

Prayer

Patient and ever-present God, thank you that you call me to a new life in Jesus Christ. Awaken me from a passive half-awake faith, and help me to eagerly respond to your call. Let me listen to your voice and open my eyes to your light. Amen.

SAYING "I DO"

From the Rule

And the Lord, seeking His laborer in the multitude to whom He thus cries out, says again, "Who is the man who will have life, and desires to see good days?" (Ps. 34:13). And if, hearing Him, you answer, "I am he," God says to you, "If you will have true and everlasting life, keep your tongue from evil and your lips that they speak no guile. Turn away from evil and do good; seek after peace and pursue it" (Ps. 34:14–15). And when you have done these things, My eyes shall be upon you and My ears open to your prayers; and before you call upon Me, I will say to you, "Behold, here I am" (Isa. 58:9).

What can be sweeter to us, dear brethren, than this voice of the Lord inviting us? Behold, in His loving kindness the Lord shows us the way of life. Having our loins girded, therefore, with faith and the performance of good works, let us walk in His paths by the guidance of the Gospel, that we may deserve to see Him who has called us to His kingdom (1 Thess. 2:12). (Prologue, Part 3)

Psalm 34

11 Come, O children, listen to me;
   I will teach you the fear of the LORD.
12 Which of you desires life,
   and covets many days to enjoy good?
13 Keep your tongue from evil,
   and your lips from speaking deceit.
14 Depart from evil, and do good;
   seek peace, and pursue it.
15 The eyes of the LORD are on the righteous,
   and his ears are open to their cry.

Contemplation

1. What word, phrase, or image from either of the two passages resonates with you?
2. What connection can you make to your own life?
3. What might God be calling you to do?

Reflection

"And if, hearing Him, you answer, 'I am he' . . ." Another translation of this text states the answer as "I do," which immediately calls to mind a wedding, where each

partner responds to the other's love and accepts the invitation to a mutual lifelong commitment. We respond in a similar way to God's invitation, having yearned for a life permeated with God's goodness and rejoicing that God has found us and called out to us.

Of course, intimacy with God has its scary side too. In response to God's unconditional love, God is asking us to change how we live and behave. We might have to refrain from vicious talk (gossip), lying, and other forms of mundane evil. We may have to think about service, doing our part to further the kingdom of God, what Benedict refers to as "performance of good works." The gospel will be our guide.

Again, Benedict's theology (at least as it is translated) may be gently questioned here. We do not earn our heavenly reward by our good works; none of us deserves God's grace by anything we have done. But God is calling us to respond to an unconditional love and share in "the way of life."

Prayer

Most loving God, you have called me into relationship with you. Give me a heart that yearns for you. Give me lips that say "I do." Help me each day to respond to your call. Amen.

TESTING THE SPIRITS

From the Rule

When anyone is newly come for the reformation of his life, let him not be granted an easy entrance; but, as the Apostle says, "test the spirits to see whether they are from God." If the newcomer, therefore, perseveres in his knocking, and if it is seen after four or five days that he bears patiently the harsh treatment offered him and the difficulty of admission, and that he persists in his petition, then let entrance be granted him, and let him stay in the guest house for a few days.

After that let him live in the novitiate, where the novices study, eat, and sleep. A senior shall be assigned to them who is skilled in winning souls, to watch over them with the utmost care. Let him examine whether the novice is truly seeking God, and whether he is zealous for the Work of God, for obedience and for humiliations. Let the novice be told all the hard and rugged ways by which the journey to God is made.

If he promises stability and perseverance, then at the end of two months let this Rule be read through to him, and let him be addressed thus: "Here is the law under which you wish to fight. If you can observe it, enter; if you cannot, you are free to depart." If he still stands firm, let him be taken to the above-mentioned novitiate and again tested in all patience. And after the lapse of six months let the Rule be read to him, that he may know on what he is entering. And if he still remains firm, after four months let the same Rule be read to him again.

Then, having deliberated with himself, if he promises to keep it in its entirety and to observe everything that is commanded him, let him be received into the community. But let him understand that, according to the law of the Rule, from that day forward he may not leave the monastery nor withdraw his neck from under the yoke of the Rule which he was free to refuse or to accept during that prolonged deliberation. (Chapter 58, Part 1)

1 John 4

Beloved, do not believe every spirit, but test the spirits to see whether they are from God; for many false prophets have gone out into the world. [2] By this you know the Spirit of God: every spirit that confesses that Jesus Christ has come in the flesh is from God, [3] and every spirit that does not confess Jesus is not from God. And this is the spirit of the antichrist, of which you have heard that it is coming; and now it is already in the world. [4] Little children, you are from God, and have conquered them; for the one who is in you is greater than the one who is in the world. [5] They are from the world; therefore what they say is from the world, and the world listens to them. [6] We are from God. Whoever knows God listens to us, and whoever is not from God does not listen to us. From this we know the spirit of truth and the spirit of error.

Contemplation

1. What word, phrase, or image from either of the two passages resonates with you?
2. What connection can you make to your own life?
3. What might God be calling you to do?

Reflection

In our day and age, it's hard to imagine young men pounding on the door of a monastery wanting to seek a life there. However, in medieval times many reasons existed to desire life in a monastery. In chaotic and sometimes violent city-states, monasteries were like small fortresses, having high encircling walls meant to keep out all but invited guests.[1] They were safe. As institutions, they were full

---

1. Mark Cartwright, "Medieval Monastery," *Ancient History Encyclopedia.* Accessed August 9, 2019, https://www.ancient.eu/Medieval_Monastery.

of educators and scholars, and there a poor young man could become literate. Monks looked after orphans, the sick and aged, and daily gave out food, drink, and alms to the poor. Benedict seemed to be concerned about those who sought to enter the monastic life for the wrong reasons—safety, a warm bed, three good meals a day, a chance to learn—and not necessarily because they were "zealous for the work of God." Making inquirers wait, testing their stability and persever-ance, was one way of assessing their motives and weighing their stamina for the monastic life.

I recognize my own impatience in wanting to pursue a path that, I think, will lead to personal or spiritual rewards. I want God to give it to me right now. In the eleventh century, Saint Romuald who, influenced by Benedict, founded the Camaldolese order and wrote his own rule, gave us good advice on this: "Empty yourself completely and sit waiting, content with the grace of God, like the chick who tastes nothing and eats nothing but what his mother brings him."

Prayer

Loving God, who opens wide your door to all who desire you, I thank you that the desire to follow you comes from you. Continue to give me the grace and persever-ance I need to keep on my spiritual path, the path to you. Amen.

STABILITY, CONVERSION, AND OBEDIENCE

From the Rule

He who is to be received shall make a promise before all in the oratory of his stability and of the reformation of his life and of obedience. This promise he shall make before God and His Saints, so that if he should ever act otherwise, he may know that he will be condemned by Him whom he mocks. Of this promise of his let him draw up a petition in the name of the Saints whose relics are there and of the Abbot who is present. Let him write this petition with his own hand; or if he is illiterate, let another write it at his request, and let the novice put his mark to it. Then let him place it with his own hand upon the altar; and when he has placed it there, let the novice at once intone this verse: "Receive me, O Lord, according to Your word, and I shall live: and let me not be confounded in my hope." Let the whole community answer this verse three times and add the "Glory be to the Father." Then let the novice brother prostrate himself at each one's feet, that they may pray for him. And from that day forward let him be counted as one of the community.

If he has any property, let him either give it beforehand to the poor or by solemn donation bestow it on the monastery, reserving nothing at all for himself, as indeed he knows that from that day forward he will no longer have power even over his own body. At once, therefore, in the oratory, let him be divested of his own clothes which he is wearing and dressed in the clothes of the monastery. But let the clothes of which he was divested be put aside in the wardrobe and kept there. Then if he should ever listen to the persuasions of the devil and decide to leave the monastery (which God forbid), he may be divested of the monastic clothes and cast out. His petition, however, which the Abbot has taken from the altar, shall not be returned to him, but shall be kept in the monastery. (Chapter 58, Part 2)

Psalm 119

[113] I hate the double-minded,
   but I love your law.
[114] You are my hiding place and my shield;
   I hope in your word.
[115] Go away from me, you evildoers,
   that I may keep the commandments of my God.
[116] Uphold me according to your promise, that I may live,
   and let me not be put to shame in my hope.
[117] Hold me up, that I may be safe
   and have regard for your statutes continually.

Contemplation

1. What word, phrase, or image from either of the two passages resonates with you?
2. What connection can you make to your own life?
3. What might God be calling you to do?

Reflection

Three promises are made when novices take their vows: stability, obedience, and reformation of life. (Other translations of the Rule transcribe the original phrase *conversio morum*—or *conversatio*—as "conversion of life" or "conversion of morals.") In my Benedictine community, we define these three vows this way:[2]

---

2. Cornerstone Community, *Cornerstone Customary for the Benedictine Community of Trinity Episcopal Cathedral* (Portland, OR: Trinity Episcopal Cathedral, 2018), 3.

- *Stability* is the promise to remain in community, even though close relationships can create interpersonal tensions, and to stay faithful to our practice.
- *Conversion of Life* is a commitment to practice the ideals of scripture and the Rule to sanctify everyday living, acknowledging spiritual transformation.
- *Obedience* is responding with deference to the abbot and others in the community and accepting the example of Jesus to seek what is best for others.

The three promises are interrelated. Stability is an act of obedience, and reformation of life empowers us to be both more stable and more obedient. In other orders, monastics also take vows of chastity and poverty, but Benedict saw these as outcomes of a conversion of life and obedience. All of the interpretations refer to one's manner of living. This change of life is indicated in the novices' final symbolic act: putting aside their own clothes and taking on the wardrobe of the monastery.

As Michael Casey[3] points out, conversion is a necessary starting point for the spiritual journey as well as a necessary device to bring us back on course when we have drifted away. And it is a gift of grace. We cannot bring it about through our own efforts. God calls out to us, and we respond by reorienting our lives to grow into the kind of person God created us to be. We change because we can do no other.

Prayer

Loving God, thank you for the grace that reached out to me, even when I was far from you. Guide my spiritual path to greater stability and obedience through ongoing conversion of life, that I may grow into the being you created me to be. Amen.

DEDICATED TO GOD

From the Rule

If anyone of the nobility offers his son to God in the monastery and the boy is very young, let his parents draw up the document which we mentioned above; and at the oblation let them wrap the document itself and the boy's hand in the altar cloth. That is how they offer him.

As regards their property, they shall promise in the same petition under oath that they will never of themselves, or through an intermediary, or in any way

---

3. Michael Casey, *The Road to Eternal Life* (Collegeville, MN: Liturgical Press, 2011), 6–7.

whatever, give him anything or provide him with the opportunity of owning any-thing. Or else, if they are unwilling to do this, and if they want to offer something as an alms to the monastery for their advantage, let them make a donation of the property they wish to give to the monastery, reserving the income to themselves if they wish. And in this way let everything be barred, so that the boy may have no expectations whereby (which God forbid) he might be deceived and ruined, as we have learned by experience.

Let those who are less well-to-do make a similar offering. But those who have nothing at all shall simply draw up the document and offer their son before wit-nesses at the oblation. (Chapter 59)

1 Samuel 1

[21] The man Elkanah and all his household went up to offer to the LORD the yearly sacrifice, and to pay his vow. [22] But Hannah did not go up, for she said to her hus-band, "As soon as the child is weaned, I will bring him, that he may appear in the presence of the LORD, and remain there forever; I will offer him as a *nazirite* [one separated and consecrated] for all time." [23] Her husband Elkanah said to her, "Do what seems best to you, wait until you have weaned him; only—may the LORD establish his word." So the woman remained and nursed her son, until she weaned him. [24] When she had weaned him, she took him up with her, along with a three-year-old bull, an ephah of flour, and a skin of wine. She brought him to the house of the LORD at Shiloh; and the child was young. [25] Then they slaughtered the bull, and they brought the child to Eli. [26] And she said, "Oh, my lord! As you live, my lord, I am the woman who was standing here in your presence, praying to the LORD. [27] For this child I prayed; and the LORD has granted me the petition that I made to him. [28] Therefore I have lent him to the LORD; as long as he lives, he is given to the LORD." She left him there for the LORD.

Contemplation

1. What word, phrase, or image from either of the two passages resonates with you?
2. What connection can you make to your own life?
3. What might God be calling you to do?

Reflection

The practice of giving your child to be separated from the family and conse-crated to God's service seems to go back to ancient times. The book of 1 Samuel tells the story of Hannah, who gave her child to Eli, the priest, for service in the temple. The child was Samuel, who later grew to become one of Israel's great prophets, who identified and consecrated young David as the one God had chosen to be king.

In Benedict's day, both rich and poor had reason to leave their children at the monastery. The nobility may have believed that monastic discipline would be good for their spoiled and unruly sons. Poor parents may have hoped that, in the monastery, their children would receive decent food, clothing, and an education.

Receiving young men into the monastery had one condition. Unlike the practice in some orders, parents could not, neither of themselves nor through an intermediary, give gifts or money to their son. Contrary to Benedict's teaching, many medieval monasteries became much like prosperous manors, and some monks had the privileges of large landowners. The wealth of these monasteries made them attractive to the sons of the nobility, and monks generally came from the upper classes of medieval society. From early in the Middle Ages, certain nunneries also were reserved to the nobility, and their lifestyle was relatively luxurious.

However, this was not Benedict's teaching or practice. He knew that money, differences in social class, and private possessions would soon cause pride among some and resentment among others. Benedict knew what he was talking about; he himself was the son of a Roman noble of Nursia. Using the early Christian community described in Acts as his model, Benedict sought to establish a society in which all things were held in common, shared among those who needed them, and no one could assume that anything was his own.

Prayer

Worthy God, let me dedicate myself to your service wholeheartedly, knowing that there is nothing that I will need except the satisfaction of pleasing you. Amen.

WHAT ARE YOU HERE FOR?

From the Rule

If anyone of the priestly order should ask to be received into the monastery, permission shall not be granted him too readily. But if he is quite persistent in his request, let him know that he will have to observe the whole discipline of the Rule and that nothing will be relaxed in his favor, that it may be as it is written: "Friend, for what have you come" (Matt. 26:50)?

It shall be granted him, however, to stand next after the Abbot and to give blessings and to celebrate Mass, but only by order of the Abbot. Without such order let him not presume to do anything, knowing that he is subject to the discipline of the Rule; but rather let him give an example of humility to all.

If there happens to be question of an appointment or of some business in the monastery, let him expect the rank due him according to the date of his entrance into the monastery, and not the place granted him out of reverence for the priesthood.

If any clerics, moved by the same desire, should wish to join the monastery, let them be placed in a middle rank. But they too are to be admitted only if they promise observance of the Rule and their own stability. (Chapter 60)

Matthew 26

[47] While he was still speaking, Judas, one of the twelve, arrived; with him was a large crowd with swords and clubs, from the chief priests and the elders of the people. [48] Now the betrayer had given them a sign, saying, "The one I will kiss is the man; arrest him." [49] At once he came up to Jesus and said, "Greetings, Rabbi!" and kissed him. [50] Jesus said to him, "Friend, do what you are here to do." Then they came and laid hands on Jesus and arrested him.

Contemplation

1. What word, phrase, or image from either of the two passages resonates with you?
2. What connection can you make to your own life?
3. What might God be calling you to do?

Reflection

Benedict's use of scripture tips his hand as to what he may have thought of priests. The Matthew text he cites ("Friend, for what have you come?") was originally from the story about Jesus's betrayal by Judas Iscariot. The New Revised Standard Version translates the quote as "Friend, do what you are here to do."

As a young man, Benedict was sent to Rome to study, but was disappointed by the decadent life he found there, even as Rome was becoming the imperial city of medieval papacy. The Roman Empire was disintegrating. Papal affairs were taken over by Germanic rulers and leading Roman families. Popes were often forced to make concessions to temporal authorities in exchange for protection. Kings appointed members of the clergy, and as a result, bishops and archbishops often came from rich families. No doubt, Benedict was familiar with priests who knew how to exercise their privilege, which would have upset the more egalitarian culture he had established in the monastery.

In Chapter 58 of the Rule, when Benedict addresses receiving new brothers into the monastery, he advises testing the spirits "to see whether they are from God." It is clear in this chapter that he extends that rule to priests as well as anyone else to wants to live in the monastery.

Prayer

Loving God, who cares for us all, watch over our community. Help me know my place in this sacred community and be a faithful servant to all. Amen.

2

⮞

LIVING IN AN INTENTIONAL COMMUNITY

BEING TESTED

From the Rule

It is well known that there are four kinds of monks. The first kind are the Cenobites: those who live in monasteries and serve under a rule and an Abbot.

The second kind are the Anchorites or Hermits: those who, no longer in the first fervor of their reformation, but after long probation in a monastery, having learned by the help of many brethren how to fight against the devil, go out well armed from the ranks of the community to the solitary combat of the desert. They are able now, with no help save from God, to fight single-handed against the vices of the flesh and their own evil thoughts.

The third kind of monks, a detestable kind, are the Sarabaites. These, not having been tested, as gold in the furnace (Wis. 3:6), by any rule or by the lessons of experience, are as soft as lead. In their works they still keep faith with the world, so that their tonsure marks them as liars before God. They live in twos or threes, or even singly, without a shepherd, in their own sheepfolds and not in the Lord's. Their law is the desire for self-gratification: whatever enters their mind or appeals to them, that they call holy; what they dislike, they regard as unlawful.

The fourth kind of monks are those called Gyrovagues. These spend their whole lives tramping from province to province, staying as guests in different monasteries for three or four days at a time. Always on the move, with no stability, they indulge their own wills and succumb to the allurements of gluttony, and are in every way worse than the Sarabaites. Of the miserable conduct of all such it is better to be silent than to speak.

Passing these over, therefore, let us proceed, with God's help, to lay down a rule for the strongest kind of monks, the Cenobites. (Chapter 1)

Wisdom 3

¹ But the souls of the righteous are in the hand of God,
   and no torment will ever touch them. . . .
⁴ For though in the sight of others they were punished,
   their hope is full of immortality.
⁵ Having been disciplined a little, they will receive great good,
   because God tested them and found them worthy of himself;
⁶ like gold in the furnace he tried them,
   and like a sacrificial burnt offering he accepted them.
⁷ In the time of their visitation they will shine forth,
   and will run like sparks through the stubble.

Contemplation

1. What word, phrase, or image from either of the two passages resonates with you?
2. What connection can you make to your own life?
3. What might God be calling you to do?

Reflection

Benedict clearly values life in community over other forms of monastic expression. Even those who live alone—Anchorites (or hermits)—do so only after being prepared in community "to fight single-handed against the vices of the flesh," and few are called to this kind of life. Benedict clearly has no use for Sarabaites, those who live according to their own rule and whose values don't look noticeably different from those of the predominant culture. Similarly, he is critical of the Gyrovagues, who wander from place to place, taking advantage of others' hospitality without making a commitment of stability.

Why are the Cenobites the "strongest kind of monks"? What is it about living in community that makes one "tested as gold in the furnace"? First, Cenobites honor their vows. They submit themselves to the instruction of a spiritual director (the abbot) and to *obedience* to each other. They promise to be dependable in their responsibilities and not to wander off when life becomes challenging (*stability*). They promise to strive toward perfection, immersing themselves in prayer and deepening their relationship with God (*conversion of life*).

Making these vows publicly and living in community promote accountability. These Christ-followers are living with others who have the same goals and who will challenge and encourage them on their spiritual journey. However, Benedict also has a message to us who are not monks: Christianity is clearly about life in community, being the body of Christ to each other and the world.

Prayer

Give me the patience, stability, and obedience to pass the test of faithfulness to Christ and his Church. Help me to be faithful to my spiritual community and to encourage and challenge others on our journey together, as the body of Christ in the world. Amen.

LIVING A HOLY LIFE

From the Rule

For if we wish to dwell in the tent of that kingdom, we must run to it by good deeds or we shall never reach it.

But let us ask the Lord, with the Prophet, "Lord, who shall dwell in Your tent, or who shall rest upon Your holy mountain" (Ps. 15:1)?

After this question, brethren, let us listen to the Lord as He answers and shows us the way to that tent, saying, "He who walks without stain and practices justice; he who speaks truth from his heart; he who has not used his tongue for deceit; he who has done no evil to his neighbor; he who has given no place to slander against his neighbor" (Ps. 15:2–3).

It is he who, under any temptation from the malicious devil, has brought him to naught by casting him and his temptation from the sight of his heart; and who has laid hold of his thoughts while they were still young and dashed them against Christ (Ps 15:4, 137:9).

It is they who, fearing the Lord, do not pride themselves on their good observance; but, convinced that the good which is in them cannot come from themselves and must be from the Lord, glorify (Ps. 15:4) the Lord's work in them, using the words of the Prophet, "Not to us, O Lord, not to us, but to Your name give the glory" (Ps. 115:1). Thus also the Apostle Paul attributed nothing of the success of his preaching to himself, but said, "By the grace of God I am what I am" (1 Cor. 15:10). And again he says, "He who glories, let him glory in the Lord" (2 Cor. 10:17). (Prologue, Part 4)

Psalm 15

1 O LORD, who may abide in your tent?
  Who may dwell on your holy hill?

² Those who walk blamelessly, and do what is right,
   and speak the truth from their heart;
³ who do not slander with their tongue,
   and do no evil to their friends,
   nor take up a reproach against their neighbors;
⁴ in whose eyes the wicked are despised,
   but who honor those who fear the LORD;
   who stand by their oath even to their hurt;
⁵ who do not lend money at interest,
   and do not take a bribe against the innocent.
   Those who do these things shall never be moved.

Contemplation

1. What word, phrase, or image from either of the two passages resonates with you?
2. What connection can you make to your own life?
3. What might God be calling you to do?

Reflection

In this part of the Prologue, Benedict tells us what he means by "good deeds," quoting extensively from Psalm 15. His definition of a holy life includes following, as much as we are able, Jesus's own model of a blameless life. Those who follow his path strive to be fair and just in their dealings with others and honest in both word and deed. They try very hard to love their neighbors as themselves, not wronging another or participating (actively or passively) in gossip. They are alert to and on guard against evil in themselves. They reverence God, giving God the credit for any goodness that they have, not themselves.

And, of course, we recognize instantly that to live this way consistently, every day of our lives, is impossible through our own efforts. Nadia Bolz-Weber reminds us that God's work in the world has always been done through sinners.[1] We take on this challenge of living a blameless life with a vision of what it means to dwell in God's tent, doing our part to establish God's kingdom on earth, understanding that it is the Holy Spirit working in us that keeps that vision alive and propels us along the spiritual path.

Prayer

Steadfast God, I acknowledge my limitations in trying to follow Jesus's example. Help me, through your grace, to lead a blameless life, and lift me up when I fall.

---

1. Nadia Bolz-Weber, *Accidental Saints* (New York: Convergent Books, 2015), 203.

Keep the vision of God's kingdom always before me as I realize that whatever good I do comes from your Holy Spirit working in me. Amen.

BUILDING ON ROCK

From the Rule

Hence the Lord says in the Gospel, "Whoever listens to these words of Mine and acts upon them, I will liken him to a wise man who built his house on rock. The floods came, the winds blew and beat against that house, and it did not fall, because it was founded on rock" (Matt. 7:24–25).

Having given us these assurances, the Lord is waiting every day for us to respond by our deeds to His holy admonitions. And the days of this life are lengthened and a truce granted us for this very reason, that we may amend our evil ways. As the Apostle says, "Do you not know that God's patience is inviting you to repent?" For the merciful Lord tells us, "I desire not the death of the sinner, but that he should be converted and live" (Ezek. 33:11). (Prologue, Part 5)

Matthew 7

21 Not everyone who says to me, "Lord, Lord," will enter the kingdom of heaven, but only the one who does the will of my Father in heaven. 22 On that day many will say to me, "Lord, Lord, did we not prophesy in your name, and cast out demons in your name, and do many deeds of power in your name?" 23 Then I will declare to them, "I never knew you; go away from me, you evildoers."

24 Everyone then who hears these words of mine and acts on them will be like a wise man who built his house on rock. 25 The rain fell, the floods came, and the winds blew and beat on that house, but it did not fall, because it had been founded on rock. 26 And everyone who hears these words of mine and does not act on them will be like a foolish man who built his house on sand. 27 The rain fell, and the floods came, and the winds blew and beat against that house, and it fell—and great was its fall!

Contemplation

1. What word, phrase, or image from either of the two passages resonates with you?
2. What connection can you make to your own life?
3. What might God be calling you to do?

Reflection

Building on rock carries the connotation of permanence and stability. I remember singing a children's Bible song many years ago that told the story of the wise man and the foolish man. The wise man built his house upon the rock. When "the rains came down and the floods came up," the house on the rock stood firm. The foolish man built his house upon the sand, and when the rains came down and the floods came up, "the house on the sand went SPLAT!" (We clapped our hands loudly as we shouted, "SPLAT.") The moral of the story was in the third verse: "So build your house on the Lord Jesus Christ."

The song was based on several scriptures that make clear that Christ is our rock (for example Isa. 28:16, Mark 12:10, 1 Cor. 10:4), and building on the rock Christ Jesus means hearing his words and living our lives according to his teachings. Here, Benedict links the two Benedictine vows of obedience and stability. And again, he reminds us that we cannot boast about anything we build, because whether it falls or stands depends on our foundation.

Prayer

Eternal God, you are the Word that has existed since before the foundation of the world and the source of all light and life. Help me to build my foundation on the rock of Christ by listening to your words and living in obedience to you. Amen.

PREPARING OUR HEARTS AND BODIES

From the Rule

So, brethren, we have asked the Lord who is to dwell in His tent, and we have heard His commands to anyone who would dwell there; it remains for us to fulfil those duties. Therefore we must prepare our hearts and our bodies to do battle under the holy obedience of His commands; and let us ask God that He be pleased to give us the help of His grace for anything which our nature finds hardly possible. And if we want to escape the pains of hell and attain life everlasting, then, while there is still time, while we are still in the body and are able to fulfil all these things by the light of this life, we must hasten to do now what will profit us for eternity. (Prologue, Part 6)

1 Peter 1

[13] Therefore prepare your minds for action; discipline yourselves; set all your hope on the grace that Jesus Christ will bring you when he is revealed. [14] Like obedient children, do not be conformed to the desires that you formerly had in ignorance. [15] Instead, as he who called you is holy, be holy yourselves in all your conduct; [16] for it is written, "You shall be holy, for I am holy. . . ."

[22] Now that you have purified your souls by your obedience to the truth so that you have genuine mutual love, love one another deeply from the heart.

Contemplation

1. What word, phrase, or image from either of the two passages resonates with you?
2. What connection can you make to your own life?
3. What might God be calling you to do?

Reflection

Preparing our bodies may be easier to understand than preparing our hearts. We don't wait until we are physically fit to begin our exercise regimen. We don't wait until we are well before we begin taking our medicine. However, we may wait until we feel full of God's love before we are ready to share that love with others, forgetting that in the Gospels, love is an act of obedience. We should not wait until the warm fuzzy feeling comes before we love our neighbors as ourselves. We mistakenly operate under the assumption that it is the feeling that motivates the behavior but, in fact, it may be the behavior—the act of obedience—that nurtures the emotion.

So what do we do to prepare our hearts? First, we remember to pray, remembering that communication is essential to any relationship, including our relationship to God. Second, we gather with others in our spiritual family in order that we may encourage each other in love and good works. And finally, in obedience, we love our neighbors as ourselves. In feeding the hungry, clothing the poor, sheltering the homeless, and visiting the prisoner, we find Christ in others and discover what God's love is all about.

Prayer

Loving God, prepare my mind for action, my body for service, and my heart to love you wholly. Give me the grace of your spirit to love others as you have loved me. Amen.

LEARNING

From the Rule

And so we are going to establish a school for the service of the Lord. In founding it we hope to introduce nothing harsh or burdensome. But if a certain strictness results from the dictates of equity for the amendment of vices or the preservation of charity, do not be at once dismayed and fly from the way of salvation, whose entrance cannot but be narrow (Matt. 7:14). For as we advance in the religious life and in faith, our hearts expand and we run the way of God's commandments with unspeakable sweetness of love. Thus, never departing from His school, but persevering in the monastery according to His teaching until death, we may by patience share in the sufferings of Christ (1 Pet. 4:13) and deserve to have a share also in His kingdom. (Prologue, Part 7)

1 Peter 4

[12] Beloved, do not be surprised at the fiery ordeal that is taking place among you to test you, as though something strange were happening to you. [13] But rejoice insofar as you are sharing Christ's sufferings, so that you may also be glad and shout for joy when his glory is revealed. [14] If you are reviled for the name of Christ, you are blessed, because the spirit of glory, which is the Spirit of God, is resting on you. [15] But let none of you suffer as a murderer, a thief, a criminal, or even as a mischief maker. [16] Yet if any of you suffers as a Christian, do not consider it a disgrace, but glorify God because you bear this name. [17] For the time has come for judgment to begin with the household of God; if it begins with us, what will be the end for those who do not obey the gospel of God? [18] And "If it is hard for the righteous to be saved, what will become of the ungodly and the sinners?" [19] Therefore, let those suffering in accordance with God's will entrust themselves to a faithful Creator, while continuing to do good.

Contemplation

1. What word, phrase, or image from either of the two passages resonates with you?
2. What connection can you make to your own life?
3. What might God be calling you to do?

Reflection

When we think about the topic of school ("a school for the service of the Lord"), we might ponder what it means to be a student. Good students are, first of all, present—they show up. These students honor the oath of stability, "never departing from the school." However, good students don't just show up; they also pay attention. They listen closely "with the ear of the heart." Good students inwardly digest (think about) what they learn, wrestling with cognitive dissonance and turning over concepts in their mind until they make sense. They also are prepared, having done their homework, faithful in prayer and study, applying the lessons they have learned to their daily life and relationships with others. Finally, good students subject themselves to the teacher and to the discipline of the classroom (the "certain strictness," the "amendment of vices," but "nothing harsh or burdensome").

The result of this instruction, Benedict promises, is an expanded heart, joy in following God's commandments, and "the unspeakable sweetness of love."

Prayer

Patient and loving God, help me to be ever mindful of the things you are trying to teach me. Help me be a faithful student in your school for service, listening to your voice and being obedient to your law, knowing that it is only through your grace that I can share in your love and serve in your kingdom. Amen.

IMPORTANCE OF THE RULE

From the Rule

In all things, therefore, let all follow the Rule as guide, and let no one be so rash as to deviate from it. Let no one in the monastery follow his own heart's fancy; and let no one presume to contend with his Abbot in an insolent way or even outside of the monastery. But if anyone should presume to do so, let him undergo the discipline of the Rule. At the same time, the Abbot himself should do all things in the fear of God and in observance of the Rule, knowing that beyond a doubt he will have to render an account of all his decisions to God, the most just Judge. But if the business to be done in the interests of the monastery be of lesser importance, let him take counsel with the seniors only. It is written, "Do everything with counsel, and you will not repent when you have done it" (Sir. 32:24). (Chapter 3, Part 2)

Sirach 32

¹⁹ Do nothing without deliberation,
  but when you have acted, do not regret it.
²⁰ Do not go on a path full of hazards,
  and do not stumble at an obstacle twice.

²¹ Do not be overconfident on a smooth road,
²² and give good heed to your paths.
²³ Guard yourself in every act,
   for this is the keeping of the commandments.
²⁴ The one who keeps the law preserves himself,
   and the one who trusts the Lord will not suffer loss.

Contemplation

1. What word, phrase, or image from either of the two passages resonates with you?
2. What connection can you make to your own life?
3. What might God be calling you to do?

Reflection

"Follow his own heart's fancy." Following one's heart is usually held to be a good thing, and many of our dreams and aspirations are worthy of following. However, laws are not usually made because people's inclinations are always to do the right thing; laws are passed to address people's potential to do wrong. Similarly, rules are necessary in a community because sometimes people do act thoughtlessly or selfishly.

Benedict talks about the inappropriateness of self-indulgent behavior or disrespectful behavior toward the abbot ("in an insolent way"). However, he holds abbots to an even higher standard, knowing that they are accountable to God for leading their communities by example as well as word. And counsel is often necessary, when the abbot will look to the senior members of the community for advice on matters that can be shared.

Prayer

O God, our "most just Judge," help me each day to follow your rule. Forgive me for my negligence and selfishness toward others, and let thoughtfulness, respect, and love characterize our life in community. Amen.

DEFERENCE

From the Rule

Not only is the boon of obedience to be shown by all to the Abbot, but the brethren are also to obey one another, knowing that by this road of obedience they are going to God. Giving priority, therefore, to the commands of the Abbot and of the Superior appointed by him (to which we allow no private orders to be preferred), for the rest let all the juniors obey their seniors with all charity and solicitude. But if anyone is found contentious, let him be corrected.

And if any brother, for however small a cause, is corrected in any way by the Abbot or by any of his Superiors, or if he faintly perceives that the mind of any Superior is angered or moved against him, however little, let him at once, without delay, prostrate himself on the ground at his feet and lie there making satisfaction until that emotion is quieted with a blessing. But if anyone should disdain to do this, let him undergo corporal punishment or, if he is stubborn, let him be expelled from the monastery. (Chapter 71)

Mark 10

[35] James and John, the sons of Zebedee, came forward to him and said to him, "Teacher, we want you to do for us whatever we ask of you." [36] And he said to them, "What is it you want me to do for you?" [37] And they said to him, "Grant us to sit, one at your right hand and one at your left, in your glory." [38] But Jesus said to them, "You do not know what you are asking. Are you able to drink the cup that I drink, or be baptized with the baptism that I am baptized with?" [39] They replied, "We are able." Then Jesus said to them, "The cup that I drink you will drink; and with the baptism with which I am baptized, you will be baptized; [40] but to sit at my right hand or at my left is not mine to grant, but it is for those for whom it has been prepared."

[41] When the ten heard this, they began to be angry with James and John. [42] So Jesus called them and said to them, "You know that among the Gentiles those whom they recognize as their rulers lord it over them, and their great ones are tyrants over them. [43] But it is not so among you; but whoever wishes to become great among you must be your servant, [44] and whoever wishes to be first among you must be slave of all. [45] For the Son of Man came not to be served but to serve, and to give his life a ransom for many."

Contemplation

1. What word, phrase, or image from either of the two passages resonates with you?
2. What connection can you make to your own life?
3. What might God be calling you to do?

Reflection

This is a hard one for me. You know the feeling. You are trying to do the right thing, but perhaps you didn't read all the instructions as thoroughly as you should have. You've stood in line for half an hour, only to have some midlevel employee tell you sharply that you should have made an appointment, or are in the wrong office, or needed to fill out a form first. I don't take that kind of correction well. I'm not good at *mea culpas*.

I am sometimes defensive when getting a performance review. My supervisor may have said ten very complimentary things about my performance, but that goal for improvement still rankles me somewhat, and I may fret about it for a couple of days.

Responding with humility isn't always easier in community, even with people you know and love. And remembering your role as a servant may take some practice and prayer. However, the peace of a community depends on its members being servants to each other and responding to our seniors in the community with deference and respect. They are God's messengers and carry the image of Christ to me.

Prayer

Forgive me, gracious God, for pride that makes it difficult for me to be a servant. May love for my brothers and sisters in community enable me to be obedient to them, honoring their place in my life. Amen.

3

EXPECTATIONS FOR LIVING IN COMMUNITY

KNOWING ONE'S PLACE

From the Rule

Let all keep their places in the monastery established by the time of their entrance, the merit of their lives and the decision of the Abbot. Yet the Abbot must not disturb the flock committed to him, nor by an arbitrary use of his power ordain anything unjustly; but let him always think of the account he will have to render to God for all his decisions and his deeds.

Therefore in that order which he has established or which they already had, let the brethren approach to receive the kiss of peace and Communion, intone the Psalms and stand in choir. And in no place whatever should age decide the order or be prejudicial to it; for Samuel and Daniel as mere boys judged priests.

Except for those already mentioned, therefore, whom the Abbot has promoted by a special decision or demoted for definite reasons, all the rest shall take their order according to the time of their entrance. Thus, for example, he who came to the monastery at the second hour of the day, whatever be his age or his dignity, must know that he is junior to one who came at the first hour of the day. Boys, however, are to be kept under discipline in all matters and by everyone. (Chapter 63, Part 1)

1 Samuel 3

[1] Now the boy Samuel was ministering to the LORD under Eli. The word of the LORD was rare in those days; visions were not widespread. . . . [10] Now the LORD came and stood there, calling as before, "Samuel! Samuel!" And Samuel said, "Speak, for your servant is listening." . . .

[15] Samuel was afraid to tell the vision to Eli. [16] But Eli called Samuel and said, "Samuel, my son." He said, "Here I am." [17] Eli said, "What was it that he

told you? Do not hide it from me. May God do so to you and more also, if you hide anything from me of all that he told you." [18] So Samuel told him everything and hid nothing from him. Then he said, "It is the LORD; let him do what seems good to him." [19] As Samuel grew up, the LORD was with him and let none of his words fall to the ground. [20] And all Israel from Dan to Beer-sheba knew that Samuel was a trustworthy prophet of the LORD. [21] The LORD continued to appear at Shiloh, for the LORD revealed himself to Samuel at Shiloh by the word of the LORD.

Contemplation

1. What word, phrase, or image from either of the two passages resonates with you?
2. What connection can you make to your own life?
3. What might God be calling you to do?

Reflection

One of the sure signs that you are getting old is when your doctor, your lawyer, your financial advisor—all the professional people you have always looked up to—suddenly look as though they are fifteen years old. The dean of our cathedral is only in his midthirties. Benedict, who was only about thirty-six when he wrote the Rule, knew that understanding and insight aren't solely the province of the elderly.

The humble servant of Christ is not overbearing in discussion, does not "pull rank" on others in the community, and does not expect others to kowtow to them. They respect the wisdom, experience, and spiritual maturity of others and know their place in the community. In Benedict's monastery, deference is given for those who have served the longest, regardless of role, and those who are acknowledged for some other "overriding consideration." As God told Samuel in another part of 1 Samuel, "For the LORD does not see as mortals see; they look on the outward appearance, but the LORD looks on the heart" (1 Sam. 16:7).

Prayer

Judicious God, who knows each one's heart, let me not judge or presume another person's worth, but serve alongside them with love and humility. Amen.

ORA ET LABORA

From the Rule

Idleness is the enemy of the soul. Therefore, the brothers and sisters should be occupied at certain times in manual labor, and again at fixed hours in sacred reading. To that end we think that the times for each may be prescribed as follows.

From Easter until the first of October, when they come out from Prime in the morning let them labor at whatever is necessary until about the fourth hour, and from the fourth hour until about the sixth let them apply themselves to reading. After the sixth hour, having left the table, let them rest on their beds in perfect silence; or if anyone may perhaps want to read, let her read to herself in such a way as not to disturb anyone else. Let None be said rather early, at the middle of the eighth hour, and let them again do what work has to be done until Vespers.

And if the circumstances of the place or their poverty should require that they themselves do the work of gathering the harvest, let them not be discontented; for then are they truly monastics when they live by the labor of their hands, as did our Fathers and the Apostles. Let all things be done with moderation, however, for the sake of the faint-hearted. (Chapter 48, Part 1)

2 Thessalonians 3

[6] Now we command you, beloved, in the name of our Lord Jesus Christ, to keep away from believers who are living in idleness and not according to the tradition that they received from us. [7] For you yourselves know how you ought to imitate us; we were not idle when we were with you, [8] and we did not eat anyone's bread without paying for it; but with toil and labor we worked night and day, so that we might not burden any of you. [9] This was not because we do not have that right, but in order to give you an example to imitate. [10] For even when we were with you, we gave you this command: Anyone unwilling to work should not eat. [11] For we hear that some of you are living in idleness, mere busybodies, not doing any work. [12] Now such persons we command and exhort in the Lord Jesus Christ to do their work quietly and to earn their own living. [13] Brothers and sisters, do not be weary in doing what is right.

Contemplation

1. What word, phrase, or image from either of the two passages resonates with you?
2. What connection can you make to your own life?
3. What might God be calling you to do?

Reflection

Ora et labora—prayer and work, Benedict's motto. In the Rule, Benedict extols the virtues of physical labor as a cure for idleness, "the enemy of the soul." I certainly find satisfaction with a physical job done well, whether it's mowing the lawn or organizing my sock drawer. Of course, in Benedict's world, prayer also counts as important labor—the *opus dei*, or work of God.

However, looking closer at the workday he recommends, the work requirement is hardly onerous. After the morning office and breakfast, the monks engaged in physical tasks until about nine or nine thirty, at which time they probably did Terce, the midmorning service. Then in late morning, the monks read. (I like that reading counted as work.) After lunch, the monks took a nap, resting (or sometimes reading) until the afternoon service of None. Then they completed their work until Vespers at about five or six o'clock. This schedule amounted to only about four or five hours of physical work, which was thoughtfully scheduled to avoid the heat of midday.

And, of course, the most important work was the work of God. Prayer is the priority in the monastery, as indicated by the seven offices throughout the day. *Ora et labora* is another example of *balance*, Benedict's principle of how monastery life—or any spiritual life, for that matter—should be lived.

Prayer

Wondrous God, who set the universe in motion and created the days and seasons, help me find your perfect rhythm within my days and weeks, making wise use of the time I have to love and serve you. Amen.

OBEYING IMMEDIATELY

From the Rule

The first degree of humility is obedience without delay. This is the virtue of those who hold nothing dearer to them than Christ; who, because of the holy service they have professed, and the fear of hell, and the glory of life everlasting, as soon as anything has been ordered by the Superior, receive it as a divine command and cannot suffer any delay in executing it. Of these the Lord says, "As soon as he heard, he obeyed Me" (Ps. 18:44). And again to teachers He says, "He who hears you, hears Me" (Luke 10:16).

Such as these, therefore, immediately leaving their own affairs and forsaking their own will, dropping the work they were engaged in and leaving it unfinished, with the ready step of obedience follow up with their deeds the voice of him who commands. And so, as it were at the same moment the master's command is given and the disciple's work is completed, the two things being speedily accomplished together in the swiftness of the fear of God by those who are moved with the desire of attaining life everlasting. That desire is their motive for choosing the narrow way, of which the Lord says, "Narrow is the way that leads to life" (Matt. 7:14), so that, not living according to their own choice nor obeying their own desires and pleasures but walking by another's judgment and command, they dwell in monasteries and desire to have an Abbot over them. Assuredly such as these are living up to that maxim of the Lord in which He says, "I have come not to do My own will, but the will of Him who sent Me" (John 6:38). (Chapter 5, Part 1)

John 6

[35] Jesus said to them, "I am the bread of life. Whoever comes to me will never be hungry, and whoever believes in me will never be thirsty. [36] But I said to you that you have seen me and yet do not believe. [37] Everything that the Father gives me will come to me, and anyone who comes to me I will never drive away; [38] for I have come down from heaven, not to do my own will, but the will of him who sent me. [39] And this is the will of him who sent me, that I should lose nothing of all that he has given me, but raise it up on the last day. [40] This is indeed the will of my Father, that all who see the Son and believe in him may have eternal life; and I will raise them up on the last day."

Contemplation

1. What word, phrase, or image from either of the two passages resonates with you?
2. What connection can you make to your own life?
3. What might God be calling you to do?

Reflection

"Do I really have to do this?" I've asked myself many times.

Benedict links obedience to humility and, in doing so, implicitly suggests that there may be two kinds of obedience. *Reluctant* obedience is not humble obedience. It comes from the feeling that the activity I am currently involved in is more important than the task my superior is asking me to do. This response certainly is reinforced by living in a culture that celebrates personal freedom and strong wills.

Immediate obedience reflects humility. I can forsake my own will and drop what I'm doing to do the more important thing God is calling me to do. This desire to please God comes with choosing "the narrow way," the road that Benedict maintains leads to eternal life. It follows the model that Jesus established. In Matthew 20:28, Jesus said, "The Son of Man came not to be served but to serve." Christ came not to do his own will, but the will of the One who sent him. It establishes for followers of Jesus the great paradox of the Christian life: "Those who want to save their life will lose it, and those who lose their life for my sake, and for the sake of the gospel, will save it" (Mark 8:35).

Prayer

Patient Father, help me to have obedience that comes from humility, knowing that my own activities and interests are good only to the degree that they further the kingdom of heaven. Help me to listen and readily respond to your leading, as it is shown to me by others. Amen.

GIVING WITH GOOD WILL

From the Rule

But this very obedience will be acceptable to God and pleasing to men only if what is commanded is done without hesitation, delay, lukewarmness, grumbling, or objection. For the obedience given to Superiors is given to God, since He Himself has said, "He who hears you, hears Me" (Luke 10:16). And the disciples should offer their obedience with a good will, for "God loves a cheerful giver" (2 Cor. 9:7). For if the disciple obeys with an ill will and murmurs, not necessarily with his lips but simply in his heart, then even though he fulfills the command yet his work will not be acceptable to God, who sees that his heart is murmuring. And, far from gaining a reward for such work as this, he will incur the punishment due to murmurers, unless he amend and make satisfaction. (Chapter 5, Part 2)

2 Corinthians 9

[6] The point is this: the one who sows sparingly will also reap sparingly, and the one who sows bountifully will also reap bountifully. [7] Each of you must give as you have made up your mind, not reluctantly or under compulsion, for God loves a cheerful giver. [8] And God is able to provide you with every blessing in abundance, so that by always having enough of everything, you may share abundantly in every good work. [9] As it is written, "He scatters abroad, he gives to the poor;

his righteousness endures forever." [10] He who supplies seed to the sower and bread for food will supply and multiply your seed for sowing and increase the harvest of your righteousness. [11] You will be enriched in every way for your great generosity, which will produce thanksgiving to God through us; [12] for the rendering of this ministry not only supplies the needs of the saints but also overflows with many thanksgivings to God. [13] Through the testing of this ministry you glorify God by your obedience to the confession of the gospel of Christ and by the generosity of your sharing with them and with all others.

Contemplation

1. What word, phrase, or image from either of the two passages resonates with you?
2. What connection can you make to your own life?
3. What might God be calling you to do?

Reflection

Not only should obedience be immediate, it should be cheerful as well. In order for our efforts to be acceptable to God, they must not be done begrudgingly or resentfully.

Is Benedict serious? For an independent, strong-willed person like myself, one might manage immediate, but being cheerful too is a tall order. That wouldn't be my natural impulse.

Benedict also makes an interesting connection between obedience and generosity, giving "with a good will." My church has a large food ministry. In addition to bags of food given almost every day to people who come to our door, about thirty volunteers provide a hot lunch to between 200 and 350 people each week. Cheerful obedience is what I see in the faces and demeanors of the food servers each week. They don't complain that they have to do menial tasks every week as they fulfill their spiritual obligation to feed the poor and welcome the stranger, but rather serve with cheerfulness and grace, interacting genuinely and lovingly with the neediest members of our community.

The secret of cheerful obedience, I think, is first gratefulness, awareness of all that God has done for us. Second, that awareness is coupled with seeing an opportunity give back part of what God has given us. Servants who demonstrate these attributes are Matthew 25 Christians, the ones who take seriously Jesus's teaching that "just as you did it to one of the least of these who are members of my family, you did it to me."

Prayer

Generous and loving God, thank you for your grace and the many blessings you have given me. Help me to serve you obediently and cheerfully, seeing Christ in the persons I serve. Amen.

WHAT WE OWN

From the Rule

This vice especially is to be cut out of the monastery by the roots. Let no one presume to give or receive anything without the Abbot's leave, or to have anything as his own—anything whatever, whether book or tablets or pen or whatever it may be—since they are not permitted to have even their bodies or wills at their own disposal; but for all their necessities let them look to the Father of the monastery. And let it be unlawful to have anything which the Abbot has not given or allowed. Let all things be common to all, as it is written (Acts 4:32), and let no one say or assume that anything is his own.

But if anyone is caught indulging in this most wicked vice, let him be admonished once and a second time. If he fails to amend, let him undergo punishment. (Chapter 33)

Matthew 19

[16] Then someone came to him and said, "Teacher, what good deed must I do to have eternal life?" [17] And he said to him, "Why do you ask me about what is good? There is only one who is good. If you wish to enter into life, keep the commandments." [18] He said to him, "Which ones?" And Jesus said, "You shall not murder; You shall not commit adultery; You shall not steal; You shall not bear false witness; [19] Honor your father and mother; also, You shall love your neighbor as yourself." [20] The young man said to him, "I have kept all these; what do I still lack?" [21] Jesus said to him, "If you wish to be perfect, go, sell your possessions, and give the money to the poor, and you will have treasure in heaven; then come, follow me." [22] When the young man heard this word, he went away grieving, for he had many possessions.

Contemplation

1. What word, phrase, or image from either of the two passages resonates with you?
2. What connection can you make to your own life?
3. What might God be calling you to do?

Reflection

When we lead a simple, purpose-driven life, there is little we need aside from food, shelter, clothes, and our tools for work. Remembering that people of different social classes came into the monastery or brought their children for care, one can easily see that those who might have finer clothing, food, or furnishings could create tension within the community. (In fact, this did happen in some monasteries.) Benedict's teaching follows the example of the early church as described in the book of Acts.

Benedict reminds us that everything we have is from God. When I visit the monastery, sleeping in a small, cell-like room and eating simple meals, I am reminded of how little I need to be at peace. In fact, I can't think of a place where I am more content, focusing my attention on things of the spirit rather than the material.

Prayer

Generous Creator, thank you for all that I have, and help me be content with what I have. Keep me ever mindful that everything I have comes from you. Amen.

COMMUNITY OWNERSHIP

From the Rule

On no account shall a monk be allowed to receive letters, tokens or any little gift whatsoever from his parents or anyone else, or from his brethren, or to give the same, without the Abbot's permission. But if anything is sent him even by his parents, let him not presume to take it before it has been shown to the Abbot. And it shall be in the Abbot's power to decide to whom it shall be given, if he allows it to be received; and the brother to whom it was sent should not be grieved, lest occasion be given to the devil. Should anyone presume to act otherwise, let him undergo the discipline of the Rule. (Chapter 54)

Acts 4

[32] Now the whole group of those who believed were of one heart and soul, and no one claimed private ownership of any possessions, but everything they owned was held in common. [33] With great power the apostles gave their testimony to the resurrection of the Lord Jesus, and great grace was upon them all. [34] There was not a needy person among them, for as many as owned lands or houses sold them

and brought the proceeds of what was sold. [35] They laid it at the apostles' feet, and it was distributed to each as any had need. [36] There was a Levite, a native of Cyprus, Joseph, to whom the apostles gave the name Barnabas (which means "son of encouragement"). [37] He sold a field that belonged to him, then brought the money, and laid it at the apostles' feet.

Contemplation

1. What word, phrase, or image from either of the two passages resonates with you?
2. What connection can you make to your own life?
3. What might God be calling you to do?

Reflection

In Benedict's time, males from all strata of the socioeconomic scale entered monastic life, rich and poor. Being able to keep one's possessions or receiving gifts from family and friends would mean the monastery would mirror and preserve the social distinctions and inequalities in the world outside the monastery. Thankfully, Benedict took his thinking from the early church, as recorded in the book of Acts. In the Jerusalem community, the followers of Jesus gave everything they had to the community, distributing "to each as any had need."

What kind of life-changing transformation and absolute devotion would motivate souls to value community over personal wealth and give everything they have to benefit others? I find that difficult to do with my own siblings, let alone members of my faith community. In the kingdom of God, it seems, material possessions count for little. Relationship with God and the well-being of those around you count for everything. The power and inspiration of the risen Christ allowed the early Christians to count everything else as unimportant.

The apostle Paul understood this. As he wrote to the church in Philippi, "whatever gains I had, these I have come to regard as loss because of Christ. More than that, I regard everything as loss because of the surpassing value of knowing Christ Jesus my Lord. For his sake I have suffered the loss of all things, and I regard them as rubbish, in order that I may gain Christ and be found in him . . ." (Phil. 3:7–9).

Prayer

Selfless Savior, who left the glories of heaven to give yourself for us, help me to understand what is of true worth and give freely of myself and my possessions to satisfy the needs of others. Amen.

KEEPING SILENCE

From the Rule

Monastics ought to be zealous for silence at all times, but especially during the hours of the night. For every season, therefore, whether there be fasting or two meals, let the program be as follows: If it be a season when there are two meals, then as soon as they have risen from supper they shall all sit together, and one of them shall read the *Conferences* or the *Lives of the Fathers* or something else that may edify the hearers; not the Heptateuch or the Books of Kings, however, because it will not be expedient for weak minds to hear those parts of Scripture at that hour; but they shall be read at other times. If it be a day of fast, then having allowed a short interval after Vespers they shall proceed at once to the reading of the *Conferences*, as prescribed above; four or five pages being read, or as much as time permits, so that during the delay provided by this reading all may come together, including those who may have been occupied in some work assigned them. When all, therefore, are gathered together, let them say Compline; and when they come out from Compline, no one shall be allowed to say anything from that time on. And if anyone should be found evading this rule of silence, let her undergo severe punishment. An exception shall be made if the need of speaking to guests should arise or if the Abbot should give someone an order. But even this should be done with the utmost gravity and the most becoming restraint. (Chapter 42)

Psalm 141

1 I call upon you, O LORD; come quickly to me;
   give ear to my voice when I call to you.
2 Let my prayer be counted as incense before you,
   and the lifting up of my hands as an evening sacrifice.
3 Set a guard over my mouth, O LORD;
   keep watch over the door of my lips.

Contemplation

1. What word, phrase, or image from either of the two passages resonates with you?
2. What connection can you make to your own life?
3. What might God be calling you to do?

Reflection

Years ago, I attended a men's weekend retreat in Arizona. On the first night of the retreat, after the evening service, we were instructed to keep silence for the rest of the evening as we went to our dorm and prepared for bed. We followed those instructions and used gesture to communicate when we needed to as we made up our bunks, completed our evening ablutions, and undressed for bed. I remember how refreshing it seemed at the time not to have to make conversation with these men who were, as yet, strangers to me and to let the profound lessons and new insights from our evening service resonate within my head. I slept very well.

Visiting the monastery, it is also meaningful to end the day with Compline (our "evening sacrifice") and then return to my room in silence, letting the events of the day sink in. Silence is the profound gift of my time there. The Daily Offices and the silent times in between them give ample time for God to speak to the heart. In the afternoon, I sometimes sit by the river, reveling in the silence. Literally all I can hear is the breeze, a cricket rhythmically chirping nearby, and the sound of a chatty magpie somewhere off in the distance. Simplicity and silence have great value, removing the distractions in life, making room for other things in one's consciousness and spirit.

Prayer

O God, who speaks not in the wind, or the fire, but in the stillness, quiet my heart and seal my lips, that I can listen with the ear of my heart to your voice. Amen.

BEING A SERVANT

From the Rule

Let the brethren serve one another, and let no one be excused from the kitchen service except by reason of sickness or occupation in some important work. For this service brings increase of reward and of charity. But let helpers be provided for the weak ones, that they may not be distressed by this work; and indeed let everyone have help, as required by the size of the community or the circumstances of the locality. If the community is a large one, the cellarer shall be excused from the kitchen service; and so also those whose occupations are of greater utility, as we said above. Let the rest serve one another in charity.

The one who is ending his week of service shall do the cleaning on Saturday. He shall wash the towels with which the brethren wipe their hands and feet; and this server who is ending his week, aided by the one who is about to begin, shall wash the feet of all the brethren. He shall return the utensils of his office to the cellarer clean and in good condition, and the cellarer in turn shall consign them to the incoming server, in order that he may know what he gives out and what he receives back. (Chapter 35, Part 1)

John 13

[4] [Jesus] got up from the table, took off his outer robe, and tied a towel around himself. [5] Then he poured water into a basin and began to wash the disciples' feet and to wipe them with the towel that was tied around him. [6] He came to Simon Peter, who said to him, "Lord, are you going to wash my feet?" [7] Jesus answered, "You do not know now what I am doing, but later you will understand." [8] Peter said to him, "You will never wash my feet." Jesus answered, "Unless I wash you, you have no share with me." [9] Simon Peter said to him, "Lord, not my feet only but also my hands and my head!" [10] Jesus said to him, "One who has bathed does not need to wash, except for the feet, but is entirely clean. And you are clean, though not all of you." [11] For he knew who was to betray him; for this reason he said, "Not all of you are clean."

[12] After he had washed their feet, had put on his robe, and had returned to the table, he said to them, "Do you know what I have done to you? [13] You call me Teacher and Lord—and you are right, for that is what I am. [14] So if I, your Lord and Teacher, have washed your feet, you also ought to wash one another's feet. [15] For I have set you an example, that you also should do as I have done to you. [16] Very truly, I tell you, servants are not greater than their master, nor are messengers greater than the one who sent them. [17] If you know these things, you are blessed if you do them.

Contemplation

1. What word, phrase, or image from either of the two passages resonates with you?
2. What connection can you make to your own life?
3. What might God be calling you to do?

Reflection

One salient memory of my visits to the monastery is seeing the monks serving each other and their guests during the midday meal, the largest meal of the day. They wore aprons and special sleeves that protected the cuffs of their cassocks as they brought trays and bowls of food to each table, allowing each person to take as much as they needed, and giving a slight bow of their head at the end of their silent interaction. As the monks and guests ate in silence, the servers cheerfully went about their tasks as if they truly enjoyed their duty. I learned that other monks were assisting the cook in the kitchen. At the end of one meal, I was especially impressed that the abbot himself rose, leaving the abbot's table, and joined others who were clearing away the dishes and table service.

In this simple act of service, the monks were following Christ's own example. Jesus himself, the very Son of God, humbled himself and became a servant. In Benedict's chapter, as in Christ's example, this service went as far as washing the feet of the other brothers.

Prayer

Gracious and loving God, thank you for the example of humility you gave to your disciples. Give me the humility to follow you by becoming a servant to those around me. Amen.

SERVICE AS PRAYER

From the Rule

An hour before the meal let the weekly servers each receive a drink and some bread, over and above the appointed allowance, in order that at the meal time they may serve their brethren without murmuring and without excessive fatigue. On solemn days, however, let them wait until after Mass.

Immediately after the Morning Office on Sunday, the incoming and outgoing servers shall prostrate themselves before all the brethren in the oratory and ask their prayers. Let the server who is ending his week say this verse: "Blessed are You, O Lord God, who have helped me and consoled me." When this has been said three times and the outgoing server has received his blessing, then let the incoming server follow and say, "Incline unto my aid, O God; O Lord, make haste to help me." Let this also be repeated three times by all, and having received his blessing let him enter his service. (Chapter 35, Part 2)

Psalm 70

1 Be pleased, O God, to deliver me;
   O Lord, make haste to help me.
2 Let those be put to shame and confusion
   who seek my life.

Let those be turned back and brought to dishonor
who desire to hurt me.
³ Let those who say, "Aha, Aha!"
turn back because of their shame.
⁴ Let all who seek you
rejoice and be glad in you.
Let those who love your salvation
say evermore, "God is great!"
⁵ But I am poor and needy;
hasten to me, O God!
⁶ You are my help and my deliverer;
O LORD, do not delay!

Contemplation

1. What word, phrase, or image from either of the two passages resonates with you?
2. What connection can you make to your own life?
3. What might God be calling you to do?

Reflection

Lord of all pots and pans and things . . .
Make me a saint by getting meals
And washing up the plates![1]

This was the humble prayer of Nicholas Hermann of Lorraine, better known as Brother Lawrence. He was an uneducated footman and soldier who, in 1666, became a Carmelite lay brother. He believed that our sanctification did not depend on changing what we did, but in doing everything for God that we would commonly do for our own sake. He strived to be in constant communion with God and to make the most menial task a prayer.

The notable thing about chapter 35 of the Rule is Benedict's attention to the spiritual, as well as the practical, aspects of service. The spirit of Brother Lawrence is reflected in Benedict's advice to the monks who serve in the kitchen, beginning their week of service with a prayer for God's assistance, repeated three times, and ending their week blessing and thanking God. One of my spiritual mentors and exemplars, like Brother Lawrence, strives to make her life a prayer.

---

1. Nicholas Hermann, *The Practice of the Presence of God* (Old Tappan, NJ: Spire Books/Fleming H. Revell Co., 1972), 8.

This is a remarkable thing. I am sadly aware of how earthbound I tend to be, and it is not my first impulse to turn my thoughts heavenward when I am engaged in a difficult or tedious task. I pray that I might learn to follow Benedict's instruction and Brother Lawrence's example.

Prayer

Ever-present God, who never turns your face from me, help me to live my life ever aware and always thankful for your constant strength and help. Amen.

Self-Indulgent Behavior

From the Rule

(Tools of Good Works)

22. Not to give way to anger.
23. Not to nurse a grudge.
24. Not to entertain deceit in one's heart.
25. Not to give a false peace.
26. Not to forsake charity.
27. Not to swear, for fear of perjuring oneself.
28. To utter truth from heart and mouth.
29. Not to return evil for evil.
30. To do no wrong to anyone, and to bear patiently wrongs done to oneself.
31. To love one's enemies.
32. Not to curse those who curse us, but rather to bless them.
33. To bear persecution for justice's sake.
34. Not to be proud.
35. Not addicted to wine.
36. Not a great eater.
37. Not drowsy.
38. Not lazy.
39. Not a grumbler.
40. Not a detractor.
41. To put one's hope in God.
42. To attribute to God, and not to self, whatever good one sees in oneself.

43. But to recognize always that the evil is one's own doing, and to impute it to oneself. (Chapter 4, Part 2)

Ephesians 4

[25] So then, putting away falsehood, let all of us speak the truth to our neighbors, for we are members of one another. [26] Be angry but do not sin; do not let the sun go down on your anger, [27] and do not make room for the devil. [28] Thieves must give up stealing; rather let them labor and work honestly with their own hands, so as to have something to share with the needy. [29] Let no evil talk come out of your mouths, but only what is useful for building up, as there is need, so that your words may give grace to those who hear. [30] And do not grieve the Holy Spirit of God, with which you were marked with a seal for the day of redemption. [31] Put away from you all bitterness and wrath and anger and wrangling and slander, together with all malice, [32] and be kind to one another, tenderhearted, forgiving one another, as God in Christ has forgiven you.

Contemplation

1. What word, phrase, or image from either of the two passages resonates with you?
2. What connection can you make to your own life?
3. What might God be calling you to do?

Reflection

In this section of the chapter on good works, Benedict writes about self-indulgent behaviors, like lashing out in anger, getting even, overeating, drinking to excess, laziness. To a great degree, the feelings that prompt these behaviors are biological. Charles Darwin believed they are left over from our animal past. They are controlled by our limbic system, the most primitive part of our brain, just above the brainstem.

As a teacher of kids with emotional and behavioral disorders, I tried not to simply punish undesirable behaviors without teaching my pupils a positive replacement. Paul, the writer of Ephesians, wisely recommends the same thing: replacing falsehood with speaking truth to our neighbors; replacing stealing with creating something to share with the needy; replacing evil talk with words that build up another and give grace to those who hear them. In correcting my own bad habits, I attempt to do the same: finding a positive replacement action to replace the self-indulgent behavior I'm trying to extinguish.

God has called us to become new creatures, bearing the image of our Creator. While not rejecting our humanness or denying our biological needs, we learn to deny ourselves, especially in those areas that interfere with our relationship with God and with others.

Prayer

Patient and loving God, thank you for the wonderful being you have created me to be. Help me to wear the image of Christ by guarding my impulses, patiently bearing wrongs, and loving others—including my enemies—as I would myself. Amen.

GOOD MANNERS

From the Rule

The juniors, therefore, should honor their seniors, and the seniors love their juniors.

In the very manner of address, let no one call another by the mere name; but let the seniors call their juniors Brothers, and the juniors call their seniors Fathers, by which is conveyed the reverence due to a father. But the Abbot, since he is believed to represent Christ, shall be called Lord and Abbot, not for any pretensions of his own but out of honor and love for Christ. Let the Abbot himself reflect on this, and show himself worthy of such an honor.

And wherever the brethren meet one another the junior shall ask the senior for his blessing. When a senior passes by, a junior shall rise and give him a place to sit, nor shall the junior presume to sit with him unless his senior bid him, that it may be as was written, "In honor anticipating one another" (Rom. 12:10).

Boys, both small and adolescent, shall keep strictly to their rank in oratory and at table. But outside of that, wherever they may be, let them be under supervision and discipline, until they come to the age of discretion. (Chapter 63, Part 2)

Romans 12

[3] For by the grace given to me I say to everyone among you not to think of yourself more highly than you ought to think, but to think with sober judgment, each according to the measure of faith that God has assigned. [4] For as in one body we have many members, and not all the members have the same function, [5] so we, who are many, are one body in Christ, and individually we are members one of another. [6] We have gifts that differ according to the grace given to us: prophecy, in proportion to faith; [7] ministry, in ministering; the teacher, in teaching; [8] the exhorter, in exhortation; the giver, in generosity; the leader, in diligence; the

compassionate, in cheerfulness. [9] Let love be genuine; hate what is evil, hold fast to what is good; [10] love one another with mutual affection; outdo one another in showing honor.

Contemplation

1. What word, phrase, or image from either of the two passages resonates with you?
2. What connection can you make to your own life?
3. What might God be calling you to do?

Reflection

It is probably an indication of my advancing age and irritability, but I often wonder at the absence of civility one sees sometimes in daily life. On the other hand, one does occasionally see a young person who offers their seat on a bus to an elder, or uses honorific titles appropriately, or comes to the aid of someone with mobility issues, or takes time to chat with an elderly person sitting alone. And then I think that the world will be left in good hands.

The theme of humility is continued in this chapter of the Rule in reference to the relationship between juniors and seniors in the monastery. Remembering that the youth in the monastery come from a range of families and social classes, Benedict has wisely addressed the issue of manners within the community. G. A. Simon[2] refers to this section of the Rule as the "code of monastic politeness" and makes the point that it is different from worldly politeness, "being wholly impregnated with the spirit of faith," that spirit being seeing the Christ in others.

And monastic politeness goes both ways. (It may not just be the youth who need instruction in manners.) He tells the youth to refer to their seniors as Father (the original word probably being closer to the Italian word *nonno*, or grandfather), but he also instructs the elders to call their juniors Brother. As Paul says in Romans, "love one another with mutual affection; outdo one another in showing honor."

Prayer

Loving God, teach me to love as you love, respecting the dignity of everyone with whom I come in contact and showing honor to both my elders and juniors. Amen.

---

2. G. A. Simon, *Commentary for Benedictine Oblates on the Rule of St. Benedict* (Eugene, OR: Wipf & Stock), 460.

Gifts and Talents

From the Rule

If there are craftsmen in the monastery, let them practice their crafts with all humility, provided the Abbot has given permission. But if any one of them becomes conceited over his skill in his craft, because he seems to be conferring a benefit on the monastery, let him be taken from his craft and no longer exercise it unless, after he has humbled himself, the abbot again gives him permission.

If any of the work of the craftsmen is to be sold, those responsible for the sale must not dare to practice any fraud. Let them always remember Ananias and Saphira, who incurred bodily death (Acts 5:1–11), lest they and all who perpetrate fraud in monastery affairs suffer spiritual death. And in the prices let not the sin of avarice creep in, but let the goods always be sold a little cheaper than they can be sold by people in the world, "that in all things God may be glorified" (1 Pet. 4:11). (Chapter 57)

1 Peter 4

[7] The end of all things is near; therefore be serious and discipline yourselves for the sake of your prayers. [8] Above all, maintain constant love for one another, for love covers a multitude of sins. [9] Be hospitable to one another without complaining. [10] Like good stewards of the manifold grace of God, serve one another with whatever gift each of you has received. [11] Whoever speaks must do so as one speaking the very words of God; whoever serves must do so with the strength that God supplies, so that God may be glorified in all things through Jesus Christ. To him belong the glory and the power forever and ever. Amen.

Contemplation

1. What word, phrase, or image from either of the two passages resonates with you?
2. What connection can you make to your own life?
3. What might God be calling you to do?

Reflection

The website I visit invites me to shop for monastery art by some of "the world's greatest living artists." Many monasteries sell objects of art—photographs, icons, posters, crosses, and medallions—in their gift shops as a way of generating income, and art dealers have jumped into the picture too.

Art has a long and important history in monasteries. Not only were Benedictine monasteries acknowledged as keepers of medical knowledge and centers of literacy throughout the Dark Ages, so too were they important nurturers of the visual arts. The sixth century especially saw an upsurge in early Christian art: illuminated manuscripts, sculpture, metalwork, and crosses.

We tend to venerate exceptional artists in both the performing and visual arts, and it is easy to see why such attention from an adoring public could go to one's head. The haughty, temperamental artist is a familiar meme in literature and popular media. For that reason, Benedict introduces a theme that runs through the Rule—humility. Gifts, talents, and graces are distributed differentially throughout the community, and a realistic appraisal of yourself as one member of a body is necessary for your spiritual health and the well-being of the community. Peter's Epistle says: "Like good stewards of the manifold grace of God, serve one another with whatever gift each of you has received." Artists, too, must take on the role of a servant in the humble way they employ their gifts.

Prayer

Wise and generous God, the giver of all good things, thank you for the abilities and gifts you have given me. Give me the spirit of a servant as I am called to share my gifts with others, remembering that there is nothing good that does not come from God. Amen.

4

THE DIVINE OFFICE

PROPER WORSHIP

From the Rule

The indicating of the hour for the Work of God by day and by night shall devolve upon the Abbot either to give the signal himself or to assign this duty to such a careful brother that everything will take place at the proper hours.

Let the Psalms and the antiphons be intoned by those who are appointed for it, in their order after the Abbot. And no one shall presume to sing or read unless he can fulfill that office in such a way as to edify the hearers. Let this function be performed with humility, gravity and reverence, and by him whom the Abbot has appointed. (Chapter 47)

1 Corinthians 14

[26] When you come together, each one has a hymn, a lesson, a revelation, a tongue, or an interpretation. Let all things be done for building up. [27] If anyone speaks in a tongue, let there be only two or at most three, and each in turn; and let one interpret. [28] But if there is no one to interpret, let them be silent in church and speak to themselves and to God. [29] Let two or three prophets speak, and let the others weigh what is said. [30] If a revelation is made to someone else sitting nearby, let the first person be silent. [31] For you can all prophesy one by one, so that all may learn and all be encouraged. [32] And the spirits of prophets are subject to the prophets, [33] for God is a God not of disorder but of peace.

Contemplation

1. What word, phrase, or image from either of the two passages resonates with you?
2. What connection can you make to your own life?
3. What might God be calling you to do?

Reflection

The *opus dei*, or work of God, is the most important work of a monastic community, as the writer reminds us here. Its importance is underscored by the emphasis on how things must be done properly. The ringing of the bell must be done by the most careful, punctual monk—and only if the abbot cannot do it himself. The chants should be led by someone who can sing properly, and the lessons read by good readers.

As a worshipper, I tend not to be bothered as much by those who make occasional mistakes (everyone makes mistakes) as by those who evidently did not prepare or who carry out their role in a cavalier fashion. I am often surprised by how moving I find services in which the music soars and liturgy flows and everyone takes their part as a sacred responsibility.

Both the Hebrew Scriptures and the New Testament speak to the sacredness of worship and the importance of everything being done carefully and reverently. For God "is a God not of disorder but of peace."

Prayer

Most Holy God, whose perfection has inspired the best in human creation, help us always to give you the best in the care and reverence with which we worship you. Amen.

PRAYING AROUND THE CLOCK

From the Rule

In the winter time, that is from the first of November until Easter, the brethren shall rise at what is calculated to be the eighth hour of the night, so that they may sleep somewhat longer than half the night and rise with their rest completed. And the time that remains after the Night Office should be spent in study by those brethren who need a better knowledge of the Psalter or the lessons.

From Easter to the aforesaid first of November, the hour of rising should be so arranged that the Morning Office, which is to be said at daybreak, will follow the Night Office after a very short interval, during which the brethren may go out for the necessities of nature. (Chapter 8)

Sirach 39

⁵ He sets his heart to rise early
   to seek the Lord who made him,

and to petition the Most High;
he opens his mouth in prayer
and asks pardon for his sins.

6 If the great Lord is willing,
he will be filled with the spirit of understanding;
he will pour forth words of wisdom of his own
and give thanks to the Lord in prayer.

7 The Lord will direct his counsel and knowledge,
as he meditates on his mysteries.

8 He will show the wisdom of what he has learned,
and will glory in the law of the Lord's covenant.

9 Many will praise his understanding;
it will never be blotted out.

Contemplation

1. What word, phrase, or image from either of the two passages resonates with you?

2. What connection can you make to your own life?

3. What might God be calling you to do?

Reflection

In the Roman world, night began at sunset, about six o'clock or six thirty, making the eighth hour of the night about two o'clock in the morning—for most of us the middle of the night. It is more common in monasteries today for monks or sisters to rise anywhere from about four to six o'clock for the service they call Vigils. (Several monasteries do not celebrate Vigils.)

Vigils is the first of seven services that comprise the Daily Office. It consists mostly of psalms, traditionally twelve, usually chanted. The service also contains short scripture readings and prayers. Traditionally Vigils began with the Invitatory, also known as the *Venite* psalm ("Come let us sing to the LORD, let us shout for joy to the rock of our salvation . . ."), which has become part of the Episcopal service of Morning Prayer.

During my short stays at monasteries, I found that observing the Daily Office seven times a day, beginning with Vigils, is very conducive to being in a prayerful state of mind all day. This doesn't mean I was always consciously praying, but I was aware of a heightened state of mindfulness and sensitivity to God's presence.

Prayer

Giver of Life, set my heart to rise early to seek the Lord and begin each day with you. Amen.

CHANTING THE PSALMS

From the Rule

In wintertime as defined above, there is first this verse to be said three times: "O Lord, open my lips, and my mouth shall declare Your praise." To it is added Psalm 3 and the "Glory be to the Father," and after that Psalm 95 to be chanted with an antiphon or even chanted simply. Let the Ambrosian hymn (*Te Deum*) follow next, and then six Psalms with antiphons. When these are finished and the verse said, let the Abbot give a blessing; then, all being seated on the benches, let three lessons be read from the book on the lectern by the brethren in their turns, and after each lesson let a responsory be chanted. Two of the responsories are to be said without a "Glory be to the Father" but after the third lesson let the chanter say the "Glory be to the Father," and as soon as he begins it let all rise from their seats out of honor and reverence to the Holy Trinity.

The books to be read at the Night Office shall be those of divine authorship, of both the Old and the New Testament, and also the explanations of them which have been made by well known and orthodox Catholic Fathers.

After these three lessons with their responsories, let the remaining six Psalms follow, to be chanted with "Alleluia." After these shall follow the lesson from the Apostle, to be recited by heart, the verse and the petition of the litany, that is "Lord, have mercy on us." And so let the Night Office come to an end. (Chapter 9)

Te Deum Laudamus

You are God: we praise you;
You are the Lord; we acclaim you;
You are the eternal Father:
All creation worships you.
To you all angels, all the powers of heaven,
Cherubim and Seraphim, sing in endless praise:
    Holy, holy, holy Lord, God of power and might,
    heaven and earth are full of your glory.

The glorious company of apostles praise you.

The noble fellowship of prophets praise you.

The white-robed army of martyrs praise you.

Throughout the world the holy Church acclaims you;

    Father, of majesty unbounded,

      your true and only Son, worthy of all worship,

      and the Holy Spirit, advocate and guide.

You, Christ, are the king of glory,

the eternal Son of the Father.

When you became man to set us free

you did not shun the Virgin's womb.

You overcame the sting of death

and opened the kingdom of heaven to all believers.

You are seated at God's right hand in glory.

We believe that you will come and be our judge.

    Come then, Lord, and help your people,

      bought with the price of your own blood,

      and bring us with your saints

    to glory everlasting.

Contemplation

1. What word, phrase, or image from either of the two passages resonates with you?
2. What connection can you make to your own life?
3. What might God be calling you to do?

Reflection

One of my former priests once told me that she had a friend who, as a daily practice, did not speak after rising in the morning until she had said, "Lord, open my lips and my mouth shall proclaim your praise." I thought that beginning the day by asking God to sanctify your lips and words was a great idea.

Reading this chapter in the Rule reinforces the awareness of Benedict's influence on the Morning Prayer still practiced today in the Daily Office. We still begin with "Lord, open my lips . . ." and the Venite (Psalm 95). We end the reading of a psalm with "Glory to the Father. . . ." We tend not to read as many psalms as monastics do. Because their practice is to read (or chant) the entire cycle of 150 psalms every week, a good number of psalms have to be read during Vigils as well as the other services.

Remember that many of the young monks may have entered the monastery illiterate, and Benedict lived several centuries before the printing press had been invented. These psalms were probably chanted from memory. During a stay at the Monastery of Christ in the Desert, I discovered that chanting is very effective in making certain phrases and verses stick in your head. One day, as I was taking an afternoon hike in the canyon, I caught myself chanting "Answer me, O God, defender of my cause; You set me free when I am hard-pressed. . . ."

Prayer

You are God; we praise you. Let every day begin with praise. Amen.

BEGINNING THE DAY
WITH THANKSGIVING

From the Rule

From Easter until the first of November let the same number of Psalms be kept as prescribed above; but no lessons are to be read from the book, on account of the shortness of the nights. Instead of those three lessons let one lesson from the Old Testament be said by heart and followed by a short responsory. But all the rest should be done as has been said; that is to say that never fewer than twelve Psalms should be said at the Night Office, not counting Psalm 3 and Psalm 95. (Chapter 10)

Psalm 95

¹ O come, let us sing to the LORD;
  let us make a joyful noise to the rock of our salvation!
² Let us come into his presence with thanksgiving;
  let us make a joyful noise to him with songs of praise!
³ For the LORD is a great God,
  and a great King above all gods.
⁴ In his hand are the depths of the earth;
  the heights of the mountains are his also.
⁵ The sea is his, for he made it,
  and the dry land, which his hands have formed.

⁶ O come, let us worship and bow down,
    let us kneel before the LORD, our Maker!
⁷ For he is our God,
    and we are the people of his pasture,
    and the sheep of his hand.
    O that today you would listen to his voice!

Contemplation

1. What word, phrase, or image from either of the two passages resonates with you?
2. What connection can you make to your own life?
3. What might God be calling you to do?

Reflection

The days start getting longer by Easter, and the sun rises earlier each day. For that reason, Benedict—ever the practical guy—advises that during this season "no lessons are to be read from the book, on account of the shortness of the nights." In an agrarian culture, the monks will need to attend to the animals and other matters at daybreak.

However, prayer is the most important work in Benedict's view and, therefore, the monks still do the rest of the service (at least twelve psalms—they still have to get through all 150 by the end of the week). The service begins with praise; the *Venite* (Psalm 95) is chanted, as it is today. It is from the *Venite* and Psalm 100 that we get the expression "make a joyful noise." (That must have been a consolation to the monks who had a hard time chanting on pitch.) The psalm instructs us to come before God with thanksgiving, to acknowledge the greatness of creation and the fact that we are part of that creation and, finally, to listen to his voice. Perhaps it was verse 7 of Psalm 95 that inspired Benedict to begin his Rule with the injunction to listen.

Prayer

Great King above all gods, remind me to begin each day thanking you for your sovereignty and your creation. Help me this day to listen to your voice. Amen.

BEGINNING OUR SUNDAY

From the Rule

On Sunday the hour of rising for the Night Office should be earlier. In that Office let the measure already prescribed be kept, namely the singing of six Psalms and a verse. Then let all be seated on the benches in their proper order while the lessons and their responsories are read from the book, as we said above. These shall be four in number, with the chanter saying the "Glory be to the Father" in the fourth responsory only, and all rising reverently as soon as he begins it.

After these lessons let six more Psalms with antiphons follow in order, as before, and a verse; and then let four more lessons be read with their responsories in the same way as the former.

After these let there be three canticles from the book of the Prophets, as the Abbot shall appoint, and let these canticles be chanted with "Alleluia." Then when the verse has been said and the Abbot has given the blessing, let four more lessons be read, from the New Testament, in the manner prescribed above.

After the fourth responsory let the Abbot begin the hymn "We praise You, O God." When this is finished the Abbot shall read the lesson from the book of the Gospels, while all stand in reverence and awe. At the end let all answer "Amen," and let the Abbot proceed at once to the hymn "To You Be Praise." After the blessing has been given, let them begin the Morning Office.

This order for the Night Office on Sunday shall be observed the year around, both summer and winter; unless it should happen (which God forbid) that the brethren be late in rising, in which case the lessons or the responsories will have to be shortened somewhat. Let every precaution be taken, however, against such an occurrence; but if it does happen, then the one through whose neglect it has come about should make due satisfaction to God in the oratory. (Chapter 11)

The Third Song of Isaiah (Isaiah 60)

1 Arise, shine; for your light has come,
    and the glory of the Lord has risen upon you.
2 For darkness shall cover the earth,
    and thick darkness the peoples;
    but the Lord will arise upon you,
    and his glory will appear over you.
3 Nations shall come to your light,
    and kings to the brightness of your dawn.

¹¹ Your gates shall always be open;
   day and night they shall not be shut,
¹⁴ they shall call you the City of the Lord,
   the Zion of the Holy One of Israel.
¹⁸ Violence shall no more be heard in your land,
   devastation or destruction within your borders;
   you shall call your walls Salvation,
   and your gates Praise.
¹⁹ The sun shall no longer be
   your light by day,
   nor for brightness shall the moon
   give light to you by night.

Contemplation

   1. What word, phrase, or image from either of the two passages resonates with you?
   2. What connection can you make to your own life?
   3. What might God be calling you to do?

Reflection

In many monasteries today, monks get to sleep in a little on Sundays. Not so in Benedict's monasteries. "On Sunday the hour of rising for the Night Office should be earlier," he writes. However, he makes allowances for human weaknesses, and specifies a Plan B if (God forbid) the monks are late in rising. Then a somewhat shorter service is called for.

   Noting the length of this chapter, Benedict seems to be more particular about how the Sunday Vigils should go. It is, for example, the first time he mentions including canticles from the books of the Prophets. It is a reminder to us that not all psalms are found in the book of Psalms. I have no idea which canticles the sixth-century monks used, but among my favorites from the Prophets are the three Songs of Isaiah. The Third Song of Isaiah (above) is particularly appropriate for morning. "Arise, shine, for your light has come, and the glory of the Lord has dawned upon you." It ends with a wonderful image of the kingdom of God, a bright and peaceful land in which violence will no longer be witnessed. It is a perfect complement to the Lord's Prayer: "Thy kingdom come, thy will be done, on earth as it is in heaven."

Prayer

Holy God, let me never lose sight of the kingdom of God, working and praying for a time when justice and peace will rule the earth. Amen.

SUNDAY PRAISE

From the Rule

The Morning Office on Sunday shall begin with Psalm 66 recited straight through without an antiphon. After that let Psalm 50 be said with "Alleluia," then Psalms 117 and 62, the Canticle of Blessing (Benedicite) and the Psalms of praise (Ps. 148–150); then a lesson from the Apocalypse to be recited by heart, the responsory, the Ambrosian hymn (Te Deum), the verse, the canticle from the Gospel book, the litany and so the end. (Chapter 12)

Psalm 150

¹ Praise the LORD!
  Praise God in his sanctuary;
  praise him in his mighty firmament!
² Praise him for his mighty deeds;
  praise him according to his surpassing greatness!
³ Praise him with trumpet sound;
  praise him with lute and harp!
⁴ Praise him with tambourine and dance;
  praise him with strings and pipe!
⁵ Praise him with clanging cymbals;
  praise him with loud clashing cymbals!
⁶ Let everything that breathes praise the LORD!
  Praise the LORD!

Contemplation

1. What word, phrase, or image from either of the two passages resonates with you?
2. What connection can you make to your own life?
3. What might God be calling you to do?

Reflection

In Benedict's mind, it seems, Sunday is the day for praise in the abbey. The morning office (Lauds) is filled almost entirely with psalms of praise, beginning with Psalm 66: "Make a joyful noise to God, all the earth; sing the glory of his name; give to him glorious praise. . . ." Psalm 62 begins with that wonderful line, "For God alone my soul in silence waits; from him comes my salvation." The canticle Benedict refers to (*Benedicite*) is also sometimes referred to as the Canticle of the Three Young Men. It begins "Glorify the Lord, all you works of the Lord, praise him and highly exalt him for ever." Its three verses glorify God for the cosmic order (heavens, stars, rain, wind, fire, and heat), the Earth and its creatures (mountains and hills, birds of the air, flocks and herds), and the people of God (priests, servants, and souls of the righteous). The last fifty or so of the 150 psalms are almost all songs of praise, and Psalms 148 through 150 are also included.

A service of morning praise is appropriate for Sunday, because Sunday is always a feast day. Even when you are not sure you're in the mood for worship, the praise psalms cannot help but lift your spirits. In the monastery, Lauds is usually followed shortly by the Eucharist service (the word *eucharistia* meaning thanksgiving).

Prayer

Mighty God, thank you for your goodness, love, and power. May my heart always be ready to praise you. Amen.

GIVING THANKS

From the Rule

On weekdays the Morning Office shall be celebrated as follows. Let Psalm 66 be said without an antiphon and somewhat slowly, as on Sunday, in order that all may be in time for Psalm 50, which is to be said with an antiphon. After that let two other Psalms be said according to custom, namely: on Monday Psalms 5 and 35, on Tuesday Psalms 42 and 56, on Wednesday Psalms 63 and 64, on Thursday Psalms 87 and 89, on Friday Psalms 75 and 91, and on Saturday Psalm 142 and the canticle from Deuteronomy, which is to be divided into two sections each terminated by a "Glory be to the Father." But on the other days let there be a canticle from the Prophets, each on its own day as chanted by the Roman Church. Next follow the Psalms of praise (148–150), then a lesson of the Apostle to be recited from memory, the responsory, the Ambrosian hymn (Te Deum), the verse, the canticle from the Gospel book, the litany, and so the end. (Chapter 13)

Deuteronomy 32 (*The Second Song of Moses*)

1 Give ear, O heavens, and I will speak;
  let the earth hear the words of my mouth.
2 May my teaching drop like the rain,
  my speech condense like the dew;
  like gentle rain on grass,
  like showers on new growth.
3 For I will proclaim the name of the LORD;
  ascribe greatness to our God!
4 The Rock, his work is perfect,
  and all his ways are just.
  A faithful God, without deceit,
  just and upright is he;
5 yet his degenerate children have dealt falsely with him,
  a perverse and crooked generation.
6 Do you thus repay the LORD,
  O foolish and senseless people?
  Is not he your father, who created you,
  who made you and established you?
7 Remember the days of old,
  consider the years long past;
  ask your father, and he will inform you;
  your elders, and they will tell you.

Contemplation

1. What word, phrase, or image from either of the two passages resonates with you?
2. What connection can you make to your own life?
3. What might God be calling you to do?

Reflection

Although Benedict lays out an order of worship in which different psalms are chanted each day, Psalm 50 seems to be a constant. Psalm 50 is the one that begins: "The mighty one, God the LORD, speaks and summons the earth from the rising of the sun to its setting." It ends: "Those who bring thanksgiving as their sacrifice honor me; to those who go the right way I will show the salvation of God." In other words, it begins by speaking dramatically of God's power and concludes by saying that the best sacrifice we can offer God is the gift of thanksgiving.

Although the psalms have a prominent place in the morning office, it is interesting to note that Benedict also specifies readings from the Hebrew Scriptures, the Epistles, and the Gospels, a tradition continued in our services today. In other words, the whole Bible is worthy of our consideration.

Prayer

Mighty God, I acknowledge your power and sovereignty. Your work is perfect, and all your ways are just. Thank you for all you have made and for all you have given me. Amen.

CELEBRATING THE SAINTS

From the Rule

On the feasts of Saints and on all festivals let the Office be performed as we have prescribed for Sundays, except that the Psalms, the antiphons and the lessons belonging to that particular day are to be said. Their number, however, shall remain as we have specified above. (Chapter 14)

Hebrews 11

[32] And what more should I say? For time would fail me to tell of Gideon, Barak, Samson, Jephthah, of David and Samuel and the prophets— [33] who through faith conquered kingdoms, administered justice, obtained promises, shut the mouths of lions, [34] quenched raging fire, escaped the edge of the sword, won strength out of weakness, became mighty in war, put foreign armies to flight. [35] Women received their dead by resurrection. Others were tortured, refusing to accept release, in order to obtain a better resurrection. [36] Others suffered mocking and flogging, and even chains and imprisonment. [37] They were stoned to death, they were sawn in two, they were killed by the sword; they went about in skins of sheep and goats, destitute, persecuted, tormented— [38] of whom the world was not worthy. They wandered in deserts and mountains, and in caves and holes in the ground.

[39] Yet all these, though they were commended for their faith, did not receive what was promised, [40] since God had provided something better so that they would not, apart from us, be made perfect.

[12:1] Therefore, since we are surrounded by so great a cloud of witnesses, let us also lay aside every weight and the sin that clings so closely, and let us run with perseverance the race that is set before us, [2] looking to Jesus the pioneer and perfecter of our faith, who for the sake of the joy that was set before him endured the cross, disregarding its shame, and has taken his seat at the right hand of the throne of God.

Contemplation

1. What word, phrase, or image from either of the two passages resonates with you?
2. What connection can you make to your own life?
3. What might God be calling you to do?

Reflection

Benedict instituted a practice that is still observed today: that is, the use of special scriptures and psalms in honor of the saint who is celebrated on that day as a departure from the regular lessons that would usually be used. The number of psalms, lessons, and antiphons remains the same, but different ones, suggested specifically for their connections to the life of the commemorated saint, are read.

No standard criteria for honoring saints existed in Benedict's time.[1] Instead, local dioceses declared saints who should be honored. Centralization of the process of declaring saints occurred within the Roman church by Pope Gregory IX in 1234. Before then, the principle in effect for designating someone as a saint was that Christ should be known more intimately through the person honored, and that the holiness of the person was evident in their Christian practice and the inspiration for those around them to act likewise.

As someone who was not raised in a liturgical tradition, celebration of saints was a new concept for me. I have enjoyed learning about the lives of these exemplars whose extraordinary faith and service serves as an inspiration to us today.

Prayer

Almighty God, thank you for the grace and power by which your holy men and women lived, many triumphing over suffering and remaining faithful even to death. Thank you for their example, and help me to take up my cross daily, faithfully following you as they did. Amen.

---

1. Report to the Episcopal General Convention from the Standing Commission on Liturgy and Music (2015).

SAYING ALLELUIA

From the Rule

From holy Easter until Pentecost without interruption let "Alleluia" be said both in the Psalms and in the responsories. From Pentecost to the beginning of Lent let it be said every night with the last six Psalms of the Night Office only. On every Sunday, however, outside of Lent, the canticles, the Morning Office, Prime, Terce, Sext, and None shall be said with "Alleluia," but Vespers with antiphons. The responsories are never to be said with "Alleluia" except from Easter to Pentecost. (Chapter 15)

Revelation 19

⁵ And from the throne came a voice saying,
"Praise our God,
all you his servants,
and all who fear him,
small and great."
⁶ Then I heard what seemed to be the voice of a great multitude, like the sound
of many waters and like the sound of mighty thunderpeals, crying out,
"Hallelujah!
For the Lord our God
the Almighty reigns.
⁷ Let us rejoice and exult
and give him the glory,
for the marriage of the Lamb has come,
and his bride has made herself ready;
⁸ to her it has been granted to be clothed
with fine linen, bright and pure"—
for the fine linen is the righteous deeds of the saints.

Contemplation

1. What word, phrase, or image from either of the two passages resonates with you?
2. What connection can you make to your own life?
3. What might God be calling you to do?

Reflection

One of the delights of Easter is to be able to enthusiastically say "Alleluia" again. *Alleluia*, or *hallelujah*, is a Middle English word, coming from Hebrew and meaning "praise Yah" (or Yahweh). It doesn't appear as often in the Bible as you might think. It appears as *hallelujah* in the Psalms, as in Psalm 147: "Hallelujah! Yes, praise the Lord! How good it is to sing his praises! How delightful, and how right!" And it appears in Revelation, as praise in heaven coming from the gathered saints and angel choirs: "After this I heard what seemed to be the loud voice of a great multitude in heaven, saying, 'Hallelujah! Salvation and glory and power to our God'" (Rev. 19:1).

In our church, on Shrove Tuesday, right after the pancake supper, children write *Alleluia* on slips of paper which they color and decorate. Then, after a noisy celebration, all the alleluias are locked away in a box that isn't opened until Easter. We give up alleluias during Lent as a kind of verbal fast, creating a sense of anticipation and even greater joy when we can use the word again to celebrate Christ's resurrection and, thereby, our salvation.

Prayer

Risen Christ, give me a heart of praise, that every day I can praise you for your salvation, glory, and power. Amen.

THROUGHOUT THE DAY

From the Rule

"Seven times in the day," says the Prophet, "I have rendered praise to You" (Ps. 119:164). Now that sacred number of seven will be fulfilled by us if we perform the Offices of our service at the time of the Morning Office, of Prime, of Terce, of Sext, of None, of Vespers and of Compline, since it was of these day Hours that he said, "Seven times in the day I have rendered praise to You" (Ps. 119:164). For as to the Night Office the same Prophet says, "In the middle of the night I arose to glorify You" (Ps. 119:62).

Let us therefore bring our tribute of praise to our Creator "for the judgments of His justice" at these times: the Morning Office, Prime, Terce, Sext, None, Vespers and Compline; and in the night let us arise to glorify Him (Ps. 119:164, 62). (Chapter 16)

Psalm 119

162 I rejoice at your word
like one who finds great spoil.
163 I hate and abhor falsehood,
but I love your law.
164 Seven times a day I praise you
for your righteous ordinances.
165 Great peace have those who love your law;
nothing can make them stumble.
166 I hope for your salvation, O LORD,
and I fulfill your commandments.
167 My soul keeps your decrees;
I love them exceedingly.
168 I keep your precepts and decrees,
for all my ways are before you.

Contemplation

1. What word, phrase, or image from either of the two passages resonates with you?
2. What connection can you make to your own life?
3. What might God be calling you to do?

Reflection

Before addressing the mundane tasks of physical labor that had to be done around the monastery, Benedict writes about prayer, specifically praise. Physical tasks had to be done to maintain the community, and Benedict considered this work to be holy work too. However, the most important work of God (*opus dei*) was prayer. The fact that other work was interrupted seven times a day to perform together the Daily Office demonstrated its priority in the daily life of the monastery.

Brother David Steindl-Rast[2] makes the distinction between "prayers" and "prayerfulness." My experience at the monastery was that joining the monks in prayer several times a day led to an experience of heightened prayerfulness throughout the day. The chanted phrases of praise from the Psalms often were going through my head. Through prayerfulness, every activity can and should become prayer. Scripture tells us to "pray without ceasing" (1 Thess. 5:17).

---

2. David Steindl-Rast, *Gratefulness, the Heart of Prayer* (New York: Paulist Press, 1984.)

Prayer

Almighty God, help me to realize that you are always near. May my prayers throughout the day lead me to prayerfulness and thankfulness for all that you have given me. Amen.

TIME FOR PRAISE

From the Rule

We have already arranged the order of the psalmody for the Night and Morning Offices; let us now provide for the remaining Hours. At Prime let three Psalms be said, separately and not under one "Glory be to the Father." The hymn of that Hour is to follow the verse "Incline unto my aid, O God," before the Psalms begin. Upon completion of the three Psalms let one lesson be recited, then a verse, the "Lord, have mercy on us" and the concluding prayers.

The Offices of Terce, Sext, and None are to be celebrated in the same order, that is: the "Incline unto my aid, O God," the hymn proper to each Hour, three Psalms, lesson and verse, "Lord, have mercy on us" and concluding prayers. If the community is a large one, let the Psalms be sung with antiphons; but if small, let them be sung straight through. Let the Psalms of the Vesper Office be limited to four, with antiphons. After these Psalms the lesson is to be recited, then the responsory, the Ambrosian hymn, the verse, the canticle from the Gospel book, the litany, the Lord's Prayer and the concluding prayers.

Let Compline be limited to the saying of three Psalms, which are to be said straight through without antiphon, and after them the hymn of that Hour, one lesson, a verse, the "Lord, have mercy on us," the blessing and the concluding prayers. (Chapter 17)

Psalm 121

¹ I lift up my eyes to the hills—
from where will my help come?
² My help comes from the LORD,
who made heaven and earth.
³ He will not let your foot be moved;
he who keeps you will not slumber.
⁴ He who keeps Israel
will neither slumber nor sleep.

5 The Lord is your keeper;
  the Lord is your shade at your right hand.
6 The sun shall not strike you by day,
  nor the moon by night.
7 The Lord will keep you from all evil;
  he will keep your life.
8 The Lord will keep
  your going out and your coming in
  from this time on and forevermore.

Contemplation

1. What word, phrase, or image from either of the two passages resonates with you?
2. What connection can you make to your own life?
3. What might God be calling you to do?

Reflection

Psalm 121 is one of the psalms chanted throughout the week at Terce, the mid-morning office. During my visits to the monastery, the three midday services—Terce, Sext, and None—were my favorite of the day. They are short services that occur at natural break times during the day. After breakfast, everyone takes some time to get ready for the day, and then walks to the chapel for Terce at about eight forty-five. After the morning work detail, we gather for Sext at one o'clock, followed by lunch. Then after some time for reading or study, it is time for None at three thirty. All services follow the same simple format: opening sentences, a hymn, the chanting of three psalms, a short scripture lesson, then the concluding prayers.

When Benedict refers to "the Ambrosian hymn," he is probably referring to one of the many hymns written by Saint Ambrose (339–397 CE). Saint Ambrose is regarded by many as the father of Christian hymnody. He composed somewhere between thirty and one hundred hymns that all had a simple melody and distinctive meter.

Prayer

Gracious and loving God, thank you for watching over your children. Help me to take time during the day to turn my thoughts toward you and praise you for all your wonderful works. Amen.

PRAISE AND OBEDIENCE

From the Rule

Let this verse be said: "Incline unto my aid, O God; O Lord, make haste to help me," and the "Glory be to the Father" then the hymn proper to each Hour. Then at Prime on Sunday four sections of Psalm 118 (Ps. 119) are to be said; and at each of the remaining Hours, that is Terce, Sext, and None, three sections of the same Psalm 118. At Prime on Monday let three Psalms be said, namely Psalms 1, 2, and 6. And so each day at Prime until Sunday let three Psalms be said in numerical order, to Psalm 19, but with Psalms 9 and 17 each divided into two parts. Thus it comes about that the Night Office on Sunday always begins with Psalm 20. (Chapter 18, Part 1)

Psalm 119

1 Happy are those whose way is blameless,
  who walk in the law of the LORD.
2 Happy are those who keep his decrees,
  who seek him with their whole heart,
3 who also do no wrong,
  but walk in his ways.
4 You have commanded your precepts
  to be kept diligently.
5 O that my ways may be steadfast
  in keeping your statutes!
6 Then I shall not be put to shame,
  having my eyes fixed on all your commandments.
7 I will praise you with an upright heart,
  when I learn your righteous ordinances.
8 I will observe your statutes;
  do not utterly forsake me.

Contemplation

1. What word, phrase, or image from either of the two passages resonates with you?

2. What connection can you make to your own life?

3. What might God be calling you to do?

Reflection

The Psalms differ in their numbering between the Hebrew (Masoretic) and Greek (Septuagint) manuscripts. Protestant translations use the Hebrew numbering, but other Christian traditions such as Roman Catholic follow the Greek numbering. What Benedict refers to as Psalm 118 becomes Psalm 119 in the Protestant Bible.

Why would Psalm 119 be recited (or chanted) at Sunday's Prime, Terce, Sext, and None offices? Psalm 119 calls us to righteous ("blameless") living. It enjoins us to do so steadfastly and with our whole heart. It encourages us to have our eyes fixed on God's commandments and diligently learn about them, praising God as we do so.

This psalm gets to the heart of our vow of obedience. We give ourselves to obedience not just so that we "shall not be put to shame," but also because our heart is devoted to following Christ, and our eyes are fixed on the model of his life and teaching. When my attention to God's commandments are more grudgingly than enthusiastically given, I take my mind back to a time when God was very real to me and my desire to follow him was strong.

Prayer

Merciful God, thank you for the contentment that comes when I keep your commandments and follow you. Keep my eyes fixed on you and my heart tuned to your teaching. You have given me abundant life. Amen.

REASSURANCE

From the Rule

At Terce, Sext, and None on Monday let the nine remaining sections of Psalm 118 (Psalm 119) be said, three at each of these Hours. Psalm 118 having been completed, therefore, on two days, Sunday and Monday, let the nine Psalms from Psalm 119 to Psalm 127 be said at Terce, Sext, and None, three at each Hour, beginning with Tuesday. And let these same Psalms be repeated every day until Sunday at the same Hours, while the arrangement of hymns, lessons, and verses is kept the same on all days; and thus Prime on Sunday will always begin with Psalm 118. (Chapter 18, Part 2)

Psalm 128

¹ Happy is everyone who fears the LORD,
   who walks in his ways.

2 You shall eat the fruit of the labor of your hands;
   you shall be happy, and it shall go well with you.
3 Your wife will be like a fruitful vine
   within your house;
   your children will be like olive shoots
   around your table.
4 Thus shall the man be blessed
   who fears the Lord.
5 The Lord bless you from Zion.
   May you see the prosperity of Jerusalem
   all the days of your life.
6 May you see your children's children.
   Peace be upon Israel!

Contemplation

1. What word, phrase, or image from either of the two passages resonates with you?
2. What connection can you make to your own life?
3. What might God be calling you to do?

Reflection

As C. S. Lewis[3] and other authors have pointed out, many of the psalms are not comforting. The psalter contains psalms of complaining, judgment, and cursing as well as those of praise and comfort. However, Benedict has chosen a collection of reassuring psalms to be said at the little offices, beginning with Psalm 119. Psalm 120 begins, "In my distress I cry to the Lord, that he may answer me." Psalm 121 is a comforting favorite of many. Many times, as I approach my favorite place of worship, I remember the words "I was glad when they said to me, 'Let us go to the house of the Lord'" (Psalm 122). Psalm 125 tells us that "Those who trust in the Lord are like Mount Zion, which cannot be moved, but abides forever." And this collection ends with Psalm 128 (Psalm 127 in Benedict's Septuagint Bible): "Happy is everyone who fears the Lord, who walks in his ways."

The path of discipleship isn't always easy, and in the monastic day of prayer and work, work and prayer, psalms of reassurance may be important. Happy are those who fear the Lord and follow in his ways.

---

3. C. S. Lewis, *Reflections on the Psalms* (New York: Harcourt, 1958).

Prayer

Steadfast God, thank you for the reassurance that you are watching over us, by day and by night. Help me always to look to you, trust in you, and follow you. Amen.

COMFORTING WORDS

From the Rule

Vespers are to be sung with four Psalms every day. These shall begin with Psalm 109 and go on to Psalm 147, omitting those which are set apart for other Hours; that is to say that with the exception of Psalms 117 to 127 and Psalms 133 and 142, all the rest of these are to be said at Vespers. And since there are three Psalms too few, let the longer ones of the above number be divided, namely Psalms 138, 143, and 144. But let Psalm 116 because of its brevity be joined to Psalm 115.

The order of the Vesper Psalms being thus settled, let the rest of the Hour— lesson, responsory, hymn, verse, and canticle—be carried out as we prescribed above. At Compline the same Psalms are to be repeated every day, namely Psalms 4, 90, and 133. (Chapter 18, Part 3)

Psalm 91

1 You who live in the shelter of the Most High,
   who abide in the shadow of the Almighty,[a]
2 will say to the LORD, "My refuge and my fortress;
   my God, in whom I trust."
3 For he will deliver you from the snare of the fowler
   and from the deadly pestilence;
4 he will cover you with his pinions,
   and under his wings you will find refuge;
   his faithfulness is a shield and buckler.
5 You will not fear the terror of the night,
   or the arrow that flies by day,
6 or the pestilence that stalks in darkness,
   or the destruction that wastes at noonday.
7 A thousand may fall at your side,
   ten thousand at your right hand,
   but it will not come near you.
8 You will only look with your eyes
   and see the punishment of the wicked.

9 Because you have made the LORD your refuge,[b]
     the Most High your dwelling place,
10 no evil shall befall you,
     no scourge come near your tent.
11 For he will command his angels concerning you
     to guard you in all your ways.

Contemplation

1. What word, phrase, or image from either of the two passages resonates with you?

2. What connection can you make to your own life?

3. What might God be calling you to do?

Reflection

The evening offices, Vespers and Compline, are prayerful, reflective, calming ways to end a busy day. In the Book of Common Prayer, Evening Prayer has the wonderful *Phos Hilaron* (O Gracious Light) that includes the lines:

> Now as we come to the setting of the sun,
> and our eyes behold the vesper light,
> we sing your praises, O God: Father, Son, and Holy Spirit.

The Psalms again have a prominent place in the liturgy. However, unlike Vespers and the other offices in which psalms are said in rotation throughout the week, Benedict clearly has favorite psalms that he wants chanted at every Compline service, the last activity of the day: Psalms 4, 90 (91), and 133 (134). These comforting words at bedtime include "speak to your heart in silence upon your bed" and "I will both lie down and sleep in peace; for you alone, O LORD, make me lie down in safety" from Psalm 4. And Psalm 91 reassures us with these words:

9 Because you have made the LORD your refuge,[b]
     the Most High your dwelling place,
10 no evil shall befall you,
     no scourge come near your tent.

Prayer

Loving God, thank you for watching over me. Thank you for your presence in my life each day and every night. Amen.

Just Do It

From the Rule

The order of psalmody for the day Hours being thus arranged, let all the remaining Psalms be equally distributed among the seven Night Offices by dividing the longer Psalms among them and assigning twelve Psalms to each night. We strongly recommend, however, that if this distribution of the Psalms is displeasing to anyone, he should arrange them otherwise, in whatever way he considers better, but taking care in any case that the Psalter with its full number of 150 Psalms be chanted every week and begun again every Sunday at the Night Office.

For those monastics show themselves too lazy in the service to which they are vowed, who chant less than the Psalter with the customary canticles in the course of a week, whereas we read that our holy Fathers strenuously fulfilled that task in a single day. May we, lukewarm that we are, perform it at least in a whole week! (Chapter 18, Part 4)

Psalm 92

1   It is good to give thanks to the LORD,
    to sing praises to your name, O Most High;
2   to declare your steadfast love in the morning,
    and your faithfulness by night,
3   to the music of the lute and the harp,
    to the melody of the lyre.
4   For you, O LORD, have made me glad by your work;
    at the works of your hands I sing for joy.

Contemplation

1. What word, phrase, or image from either of the two passages resonates with you?
2. What connection can you make to your own life?
3. What might God be calling you to do?

Reflection

In regard to chanting the psalms, it seems Benedict is saying that, in the end, it doesn't matter when or in which order you do it, just do it. I think this is particularly good advice for the beginner (and we are all beginners). In learning theory, there is the principle of *gradual approximations*, or not expecting immediate mastery of a new skill or routine. Rather, each step toward the goal should be rewarded, encouraging the learner along the path to eventual success.

So, Benedict says to his monks, if you can't read all 150 psalms every day, as the early fathers did, at least aim for reading all 150 in a week. To those of us today who are not monks and do not gather for prayer seven times a day, I think he would say read one or two psalms a day. The Daily Office Lectionary in the Book of Common Prayer lays out a plan where, during morning and evening prayer, the entire psalm cycle is read in about seven weeks. I am a beginner; I will do what I can with God's help.

Prayer

God of Light, keep me diligent in my spiritual practice. And as I read the Psalms, let them stir my thoughts and lift my heart towards you. Amen.

5

PERSONAL PIETY

LOVING GOD AND LOVING OTHERS

From the Rule (*The Tools of Good Works*)

1. In the first place, to love the Lord God with the whole heart, the whole soul, the whole strength.
2. Then, one's neighbor as oneself.
3. Then not to murder.
4. Not to commit adultery.
5. Not to steal.
6. Not to covet.
7. Not to bear false witness.
8. To honor all (1 Peter 2:17).
9. And not to do to another what one would not have done to oneself.
10. To deny oneself in order to follow Christ.
11. To chastise the body.
12. Not to become attached to pleasures.
13. To love fasting.
14. To relieve the poor.
15. To clothe the naked.
16. To visit the sick.
17. To bury the dead.
18. To help in trouble.
19. To console the sorrowing.
20. To become a stranger to the world's ways.
21. To prefer nothing to the love of Christ. (Chapter 4, Part 1)

1 Peter 2

[11] Beloved, I urge you as aliens and exiles to abstain from the desires of the flesh that wage war against the soul. [12] Conduct yourselves honorably among the Gentiles, so that, though they malign you as evildoers, they may see your honorable deeds and glorify God when he comes to judge.

[13] For the Lord's sake accept the authority of every human institution, whether of the emperor as supreme, [14] or of governors, as sent by him to punish those who do wrong and to praise those who do right. [15] For it is God's will that by doing right you should silence the ignorance of the foolish. [16] As servants of God, live as free people, yet do not use your freedom as a pretext for evil. [17] Honor everyone. Love the family of believers. Fear God.

Contemplation

1. What word, phrase, or image from either of the two passages resonates with you?
2. What connection can you make to your own life?
3. What might God be calling you to do?

Reflection

Benedict borrows the first set of good works generously from other familiar sources. The Ten Commandments are there (don't murder, don't commit adultery, don't steal, and so on). Christ's two greatest commandments are there (love the Lord your God, and love your neighbor as yourself). The Golden Rule and the Matthew 25 commandments are there as well (relieve the poor, clothe the naked, visit the sick, help those in trouble). He includes penitential practices (chastise the body, love fasting).

Probably the most striking to me, however, and unique in lists of good works, are Benedict's guidelines for setting oneself apart for God's service: that is, not being attached to pleasures, denying oneself, becoming a stranger to the world's ways, and preferring nothing to the love of Christ. There are not too many things in my comfortable life to which I have not become attached. Would I give these up to follow Christ?

Prayer

Thank you for the life I live and the many comforts and pleasures I enjoy. As your servant, help me to live free but ever conscious and obedient to your will. Among all the world's distractions, help me to prefer nothing to your love. Amen.

Living with Awareness

From the Rule (*The Tools of Good Works, continued*)

44. To fear the Day of Judgment.

45. To be in dread of hell.

46. To desire eternal life with all the passion of the spirit.

47. To keep death daily before one's eyes.

48. To keep constant guard over the actions of one's life.

49. To know for certain that God sees one everywhere.

50. When evil thoughts come into one's heart, to dash them against Christ immediately.

51. And to manifest them to one's spiritual guardian.

52. To guard one's tongue against evil and depraved speech.

53. Not to love much talking.

54. Not to speak useless words or words that move to laughter.

55. Not to love much or boisterous laughter.

56. To listen willingly to holy reading.

57. To devote oneself frequently to prayer.

58. Daily in one's prayers, with tears and sighs, to confess one's past sins to God, and to amend them for the future.

59. Not to fulfill the desires of the flesh; to hate one's own will.

60. To obey in all things the commands of the Abbot or Abbess even though they (which God forbid) should act otherwise, mindful of the Lord's precept, "Do what they say, but not what they do."

61. Not to wish to be called holy before one is holy; but first to be holy, that one may be truly so called. (Chapter 4, Part 3)

1 Peter 1

[13] Therefore prepare your minds for action; discipline yourselves; set all your hope on the grace that Jesus Christ will bring you when he is revealed. [14] Like obedient children, do not be conformed to the desires that you formerly had in ignorance. [15] Instead, as he who called you is holy, be holy yourselves in all your conduct; [16] for it is written, "You shall be holy, for I am holy."

Contemplation

1. What word, phrase, or image from either of the two passages resonates with you?
2. What connection can you make to your own life?
3. What might God be calling you to do?

Reflection

Benedict continues his list of good works with a chilling interpretation of God's righteousness. He draws the distinction between the fear of hell and desire of eternal life in vivid medieval language. Modern Christians have a harder time grappling with such stark concepts of heaven and hell, but few of us have a hard time looking at the world and not keenly understanding the difference between good and evil. The God who dwells in us certainly judges our thoughts and actions. I run those tapes in my mind almost every day.

However, we must also remember that when the Psalms refer to judgment, they almost always refer to social justice: God bringing down the proud and lifting up the lowly. (Perhaps that is why Benedict exhorts us not to wish to be called holy before we are holy.) Psalm 75 assures us that God will judge with equity.

So how then should we live? The messages that resonate most for me are, first, as Benedict exhorts us, to keep death daily before my eyes. As I get older, it becomes easier to value the time I have and realize the importance of making the most of every day. As W. H. Auden wrote, "Life is the destiny you are bound to refuse until you have consented to die."[1]

Also meaningful is Benedict's revelation that "God sees one everywhere." Or in the words of the liturgy, "To you all hearts are open, all desires known, and from you no secrets are hid." Finally, Benedict underscores the importance of responding to God's unwavering presence by leading a circumspect life, listening to holy reading, devoting oneself to prayer, and living in humble obedience.

Prayer

Ever-present God, help me to be continually aware that nothing is hidden from you. Keeping my mortality in mind, bring me to holiness, casting at your feet those thoughts and impulses that are sinful and learning to love the things that you love. Amen.

---

1. W. H. Auden, "For the Time Being," in *W.H. Auden Collected Poems*, ed. Edward Mendelson (New York: Modern Library/Random House, 1976).

BEING ON GUARD

From the Rule

We must be on our guard, therefore, against evil desires, for death lies close by the gate of pleasure. Hence the Scripture gives this command: "Go not after your concupiscences" (Sir. 18:30).

So therefore, since the eyes of the Lord observe the good and the evil (Prov. 15:3) and the Lord is always looking down from heaven on the children of earth "to see if there be anyone who understands and seeks God" (Ps. 14:2), and since our deeds are daily, day and night, reported to the Lord by the Angels assigned to us, we must constantly beware, brethren, as the Prophet says in the Psalm, lest at any time God see us falling into evil ways and becoming unprofitable (Ps. 14:3); and lest, having spared us for the present because in His kindness He awaits our reformation, He says to us in the future, "These things you did, and I held My peace" (Ps. 50:21). (Chapter 7, Part 5)

Psalm 14

1 Fools say in their hearts, "There is no God."
They are corrupt, they do abominable deeds;
there is no one who does good.
2 The LORD looks down from heaven on humankind
to see if there are any who are wise,
who seek after God.
3 They have all gone astray, they are all alike perverse;
there is no one who does good,
no, not one.
4 Have they no knowledge, all the evildoers
who eat up my people as they eat bread,
and do not call upon the LORD?
5 There they shall be in great terror,
for God is with the company of the righteous.

Contemplation

1. What word, phrase, or image from either of the two passages resonates with you?
2. What connection can you make to your own life?
3. What might God be calling you to do?

Reflection

"Concupiscences" is such an interesting, anachronistic word—so full of sixteenth-century judgment. Other translations read "lusts" or "base desires." Benedict tells us not to pursue them. "Concupiscence" really means any excessively strong desire, although it is usually interpreted to be sexual desire. It appears from this context that Benedict is taking the broader interpretation. He writes of the ever-watchful God looking down from heaven to see if we are staying on the right track (not "falling into evil ways and becoming unprofitable"). He wants followers who are wise, as the psalm says, who understand and seek after God.

Benedict is saying that we should be alert to anything that distracts us or takes us off the spiritual path. We cannot wantonly pursue our own desires and, at the same time, live a life of simplicity and humility. However, he does not paint a picture of a punitive, judgmental God. Instead he speaks of a God who holds his peace and patiently waits for our reformation, our *conversatio*—change of life.

Prayer

Patient and loving God, you know my desires and those things that distract me from my true life's purpose. Keep my footsteps on the right path and give me the humility and perseverance to take up your cross and follow only you. Amen.

GOD IS EVERYWHERE

From the Rule

We believe that the divine presence is everywhere and that "the eyes of the Lord are looking on the good and the evil in every place" (Prov. 15:3). But we should believe this especially without any doubt when we are assisting at the Work of God. To that end let us be mindful always of the Prophet's words, "Serve the Lord in fear" (Ps. 2:11) and again "Sing praises wisely" (Ps. 46[47]:8) and "In the sight of the Angels I will sing praise to You" (Ps. 137[138]:1). Let us therefore consider how we ought to conduct ourselves in sight of the Godhead and of His Angels, and let us take part in the psalmody in such a way that our mind may be in harmony with our voice. (Chapter 19)

Psalm 138

1 I give you thanks, O LORD, with my whole heart;
before the gods I sing your praise;

2 I bow down toward your holy temple
and give thanks to your name for your steadfast love and your faithfulness;
for you have exalted your name and your word above everything.
3 On the day I called, you answered me,
you increased my strength of soul.
4 All the kings of the earth shall praise you, O Lord,
for they have heard the words of your mouth.
5 They shall sing of the ways of the Lord,
for great is the glory of the Lord.
6 For though the Lord is high, he regards the lowly;
but the haughty he perceives from far away.
7 Though I walk in the midst of trouble,
you preserve me against the wrath of my enemies;
you stretch out your hand, and your right hand delivers me.
8 The Lord will fulfill his purpose for me;
your steadfast love, O Lord, endures forever.
Do not forsake the work of your hands.

Contemplation

1. What word, phrase, or image from either of the two passages resonates with you?
2. What connection can you make to your own life?
3. What might God be calling you to do?

Reflection

"We believe that the divine presence is everywhere," Benedict says. God is there in our work, in our sleep, at our meal, and with us during prayer. And, he says, God is especially present when we are assisting with the Work of God (*opus dei*).

Sadly, we are not always conscious of that reality. Although we occasionally have transcendent experiences in those "thin places" the Celts talked about, we don't always feel God's presence, even in worship. Sometimes our minds wander. We are distracted by the celebrant's tone of voice, the mispronunciation of a word, the person coughing behind us. We are thinking about the person we forgot to call, a deadline we need to meet the next day, or the thoughtless response from a person we considered a friend.

The challenge for me is being present, knowing that God expects something from me in the collective work of prayer. Benedict tells us to "serve the Lord in fear" and "sing praises *wisely*" (which I interpret to mean *mindfully*). Perhaps I can achieve this by remembering what God is bringing to the encounter: "On the day I called, you answered me; you increased my strength of soul."

Prayer

Patient and loving God, keep me always mindful of your presence. Let me always be thankful for your steadfast love and faithfulness. Amen.

REFRAINING FROM SPEAKING

From the Rule

Let us do what the Prophet says: "I said, 'I will guard my ways, that I may not sin with my tongue. I have set a guard to my mouth.' I was mute and was humbled, and kept silence even from good things" (Ps. 39:2–3). Here the Prophet shows that if the spirit of silence ought to lead us at times to refrain even from good speech, so much the more ought the punishment for sin make us avoid evil words. Therefore, since the spirit of silence is so important, permission to speak should rarely be granted even to perfect disciples, even though it be for good, holy edifying conversation; for it is written, "In much speaking you will not escape sin" (Prov. 10:19), and in another place, "Death and life are in the power of the tongue" (Prov. 18:21). For speaking and teaching belong to the master; the disciple's part is to be silent and to listen. And for that reason if anything has to be asked of the Superior, it should be asked with all the humility and submission inspired by reverence. But as for coarse jests and idle words or words that move to laughter, these we condemn everywhere with a perpetual ban, and for such conversation we do not permit a disciple to open his mouth. (Chapter 6)

Proverbs 10

¹¹ The mouth of the righteous is a fountain of life,
   but the mouth of the wicked conceals violence.
¹² Hatred stirs up strife,
   but love covers all offenses.
¹³ On the lips of one who has understanding wisdom is found,
   but a rod is for the back of one who lacks sense.
¹⁴ The wise lay up knowledge,
   but the babbling of a fool brings ruin near. . . .
¹⁹ When words are many, transgression is not lacking,
   but the prudent are restrained in speech.

Contemplation

1. What word, phrase, or image from either of the two passages resonates with you?
2. What connection can you make to your own life?
3. What might God be calling you to do?

Reflection

Knowing when to keep silent and listen when you have lots to say has to be one of the very hardest things to do. Looking back on my life, my biggest regrets are the impetuous, insensitive things I've said to others, sometimes being thoughtless, if not intentionally cruel, and sometimes in a poor attempt at humor. I can't take those words back. Benedict is right to caution us in our speech.

The Epistle of James has much to say about control of the tongue. "With it we bless the Lord and Father, and with it we curse those who are made in the likeness of God," James writes (James 3:9), and he concludes, "This ought not to be so." James likens the tongue to a fire that can set ablaze a whole forest.

However, Benedict is not just talking about negative speech. He links restraint of speech to humility, and recommends that there are times when we should refrain even from good speech. "The disciple's part is to be silent and listen." I find that when I have lots to say, I'm not very good at listening. Rather I'm looking for my opportunity to jump into the conversation or mentally rehearsing how I want to express my idea. I know that I cannot be confident of my spiritual maturity until I develop a holy spirit of silent deference and the skill of deep listening.

Prayer

Holy and patient God, give me the humility and wisdom to know when to guard my tongue. Teach me to listen, and give me the holy spirit of silence. Amen.

HOW TO PRAY

From the Rule

When we wish to suggest our wants to men of high station, we do not presume to do so except with humility and reverence. How much the more, then, are complete humility and pure devotion necessary in supplication of the Lord who is God of the universe! And let us be assured that it is not in saying a great deal that we shall be heard (Matt. 6:7), but in purity of heart and in tears of compunction. Our prayer, therefore, ought to be short and pure, unless it happens to be prolonged by an inspiration of divine grace. In community, however, let prayer be very short, and when the Superior gives the signal let all rise together. (Chapter 20)

Matthew 6

[5] "And whenever you pray, do not be like the hypocrites; for they love to stand and pray in the synagogues and at the street corners, so that they may be seen by others. Truly I tell you, they have received their reward. [6] But whenever you pray, go into your room and shut the door and pray to your Father who is in secret; and your Father who sees in secret will reward you. [7] "When you are praying, do not heap up empty phrases as the Gentiles do; for they think that they will be heard because of their many words. [8] Do not be like them, for your Father knows what you need before you ask him."

Contemplation

1. What word, phrase, or image from either of the two passages resonates with you?
2. What connection can you make to your own life?
3. What might God be calling you to do?

Reflection

I was raised in a church in which one indication of a person's piety was his or her ability to give long, passionate, eloquent prayers. When faithful members would get together in restaurants, no one would think to touch their food until the most pious among them would say a bold, embarrassingly long prayer that often silenced conversation at nearby tables. Prayer was a conspicuous act of piety.

However, Christ taught we shouldn't pray to be seen or heard by others, but that we should pray privately and humbly. And Benedict adds that, when there is an occasion for a collective prayer (and it is okay to pray together before a meal), the prayer should be short. God knows our hearts. There is nothing we can tell him that he doesn't already understand.

Prayer

Loving God, you know my heart and the desires of my heart. Let me approach you in reverence and humility when I come to you in prayer. Amen.

CONFESSING ERRORS

From the Rule

When anyone has made a mistake while reciting a Psalm, a responsory, an anti-phon or a lesson, if he does not humble himself there before all by making a sat-isfaction, let him undergo a greater punishment because he would not correct by humility what he did wrong through carelessness. (Chapter 45)

Philippians 2

⁵ Let the same mind be in you that was[a] in Christ Jesus, ⁶ who, though he was in the form of God, did not regard equality with God as something to be exploited, ⁷ but emptied himself, taking the form of a slave, being born in human likeness. And being found in human form, ⁸ he humbled himself and became obedient to the point of death—even death on a cross. ⁹ Therefore God also highly exalted him and gave him the name that is above every name.

Contemplation

1. What word, phrase, or image from either of the two passages resonates with you?
2. What connection can you make to your own life?
3. What might God be calling you to do?

Reflection

Confession of an error or, failing that, punishment for a mistake in the liturgy is Benedict's way of emphasizing the seriousness and sacredness of the *opus dei*.

While attending services at the abbey in Mt. Angel, Oregon, I noticed that occasionally a monk would step out of his place and reverence the cross. I asked the guest master the meaning of that gesture, and he explained that the monk had made a mistake while intoning the chant and was acknowledging his error before the community. I experienced a similar thing when I sang in a very fine choir. I noticed occasionally singers would quickly raise their hand to acknowl-edge they had made a mistake while reading the music. (I never had a secure enough ego as an untrained singer to acknowledge when I made mistakes, which were frequent.)

It does take humility to acknowledge a mistake before the community you're with. It helps if you are secure in the knowledge that, despite your mistakes, you are loved and valued within that community. My challenge is, in the words of the apostle Paul, to acquire "the same mindset as Christ Jesus," humbling myself before others, as an act of obedience.

Prayer

Ever-loving God, who is quicker to forgive than to punish, teach me to humble myself in my acts of service to others and accept the consequences of my mistakes, knowing that your love will uphold and strengthen me. Amen.

OTHER FAULTS

From the Rule

When anyone is engaged in any sort of work, whether in the kitchen, in the cellar, in a shop, in the bakery, in the garden, while working at some craft, or in any other place, and he commits some fault, or breaks something, or loses something, or transgresses in any other way whatsoever, if he does not come immediately before the Abbot and the community of his own accord to make satisfaction and confess his fault, then when it becomes known through another, let him be subjected to a more severe correction.

But if the sin-sickness of the soul is a hidden one, let him reveal it only to the Abbot or to a spiritual father, who knows how to cure his own and others' wounds without exposing them and making them public. (Chapter 46)

Psalm 32

1 Happy are those whose transgression is forgiven,
   whose sin is covered.
2 Happy are those to whom the LORD imputes no iniquity,
   and in whose spirit there is no deceit.
3 While I kept silence, my body wasted away
   through my groaning all day long.
4 For day and night your hand was heavy upon me;
   my strength was dried up[a] as by the heat of summer. *Selah*
5 Then I acknowledged my sin to you,
   and I did not hide my iniquity;
   I said, "I will confess my transgressions to the LORD,"
   and you forgave the guilt of my sin.

Contemplation

1. What word, phrase, or image from either of the two passages resonates with you?
2. What connection can you make to your own life?
3. What might God be calling you to do?

Reflection

As I get older, I do think about my life more. While, all in all, I am happy with my accomplishments and the way that things turned out, I do have a few regrets. Those center primarily on the people I hurt along the way and the sins I did not confess. The psalmist says, "While I kept silent, my bones wasted away. . . . Your hand was heavy upon me. . . . My strength was sapped." Guilt over unconfessed sin takes its toll.

So Benedict isn't being controlling or punitive when he says to come forward immediately and make satisfaction. He knows that it is in the best interest of the offender's spiritual well-being as well as the health of the community.

Then there is the "sin-sickness of the soul," for which public confession would not be edifying and may be very difficult to explain to others. That is where the abbot, in the role of shepherd or spiritual guide, will seek opportunities to counsel members who are in emotional or spiritual distress or whose behaviors deviate from the Rule and scriptural teaching. As H. Van der Looy says in *Rule for a New Brother*:[2]

> Let the superior be for you
> as a presence of the lord,
> not because of human qualities
> and leadership,
> but for the sake of the superior's special calling
> and grace.

Prayer

Jesus, our good shepherd, who leads us on the right path and gently guides us back into the fold, help us always have the wisdom and courage to bring to you our faults and failings for your wise counsel and healing touch. Amen.

---

2. H. Van der Looy, *Rule for a New Brother* (Springfield, IL: Templegate, 1973), 34.

READING TO UNDERSTAND

From the Rule

From the first of October until the beginning of Lent, let them apply themselves to reading up to the end of the second hour. At the second hour let Terce be said, and then let all labor at the work assigned them until None. At the first signal for the Hour of None let everyone break off from his work and hold himself ready for the sounding of the second signal. After the meal let them apply themselves to their reading or to the Psalms.

On the days of Lent, from morning until the end of the third hour let them apply themselves to their reading, and from then until the end of the tenth hour let them do the work assigned them. And in these days of Lent they shall each receive a book from the library, which they shall read straight through from the beginning. These books are to be given out at the beginning of Lent.

But certainly one or two of the seniors should be deputed to go about the monastery at the hours when the brethren are occupied in reading and see that there be no lazy brother who spends his time in idleness or gossip and does not apply himself to the reading, so that he is not only unprofitable to himself but also distracts others. If such a one be found (which God forbid), let him be corrected once and a second time; if he does not amend, let him undergo the punishment of the Rule in such a way that the rest may take warning.

Moreover, one brother shall not associate with another at unseasonable hours.

On Sundays, let all occupy themselves in reading, except those who have been appointed to various duties. But if anyone should be so negligent and shiftless that he will not or cannot study or read, let him be given some work to do so that he will not be idle.

Weak or sickly brethren should be assigned a task or craft of such a nature as to keep them from idleness and at the same time not to overburden them or drive them away with excessive toil. Their weakness must be taken into consideration by the Abbot. (Chapter 48, Part 2)

Ephesians 3

This is the reason that I Paul am a prisoner for Christ Jesus for the sake of you Gentiles— [2] for surely you have already heard of the commission of God's grace that was given me for you, [3] and how the mystery was made known to me by revelation, as I wrote above in a few words, [4] a reading of which will enable you to perceive my understanding of the mystery of Christ. [5] In former generations this mystery was not made known to humankind, as it has now been revealed to his holy apostles and prophets by the Spirit: [6] that is, the Gentiles have become fellow heirs, members of the same body, and sharers in the promise in Christ Jesus through the gospel. . . . [16] I pray that, according to the riches of his glory, he may grant that you may be strengthened in your inner being with power through his Spirit, [17] and that Christ may dwell in your hearts through faith, as you are being rooted and grounded in love. [18] I pray that you may have the power to comprehend, with all the saints, what is the breadth and length and height and depth, [19] and to know the love of Christ that surpasses knowledge, so that you may be filled with all the fullness of God.

Contemplation

1. What word, phrase, or image from either of the two passages resonates with you?
2. What connection can you make to your own life?
3. What might God be calling you to do?

Reflection

Maryanne Wolf's remarkable book *Proust and the Squid* begins with these words:

> We were never born to read. Human beings invented reading only a few thousand years ago. And with this invention, we rearranged the very organization of our brain, which in turn expanded the ways we were able to think, which altered the intellectual evolution of our species. Reading is one of the single most remarkable inventions in history. . . .[3]

In an age of wide-spread illiteracy, reading was an invention that Benedict embraced, and he required it of all his monks. Benedict was a well-educated man who, I suspect, believed that reading was as important to a brother's spiritual development as it was to his intellectual development. Only when someone would not or could not read would they be assigned another more menial task or a craft. In his epilogue to the Rule (Chapter 73), he challenges the reader to study the "divinely inspired books" of the Old and New Testaments and the extensive writings of the early fathers.

I think about the impact of contemporary Christian writers and thinkers on my spiritual formation. After reading Esther de Waal's *Seeking Life*,[4] I will never look at baptism or the Easter Vigil the same way again. Michael Casey[5] taught me

---

3. Maryanne Wolf, *Proust and the Squid* (New York: HarperCollins, 2007), 3.

4. Esther de Waal, *Seeking Life* (Collegeville, MN: Liturgical Press, 2009).

5. Michael Casey, *Grace: On the Journey to God* (Brewster, MA: Paraclete Press, 2018).

an appreciation for the "grace of discontinuity," a sometimes disruptive change in life circumstances that leads to a spiritual transformation. We read to understand more about the "mystery of Christ."

Prayer

Wise and loving God, thank you for the enlightened men and women who have shared their insights through writing. Sustain in me a desire to learn and apply their wisdom. Amen.

OFFERING TO GOD WITH JOY

From the Rule

Although the life of a monk ought to have about it at all times the character of a Lenten observance, yet since few have the virtue for that, we therefore urge that during the actual days of Lent the brethren keep their lives most pure and at the same time wash away during these holy days all the negligences of other times. And this will be worthily done if we restrain ourselves from all vices and give ourselves up to prayer with tears, to reading, to compunction of heart and to abstinence.

During these days, therefore, let us increase somewhat the usual burden of our service, as by private prayers and by abstinence in food and drink. Thus, everyone of his own will may offer God "with joy of the Holy Spirit" (1 Thess. 1:6) something above the measure required of him. From his body, that is he may withhold some food, drink, sleep, talking and jesting; and with the joy of spiritual desire he may look forward to holy Easter.

Let each one, however, suggest to his Abbot what it is that he wants to offer, and let it be done with his blessing and approval. For anything done without the permission of the spiritual father will be imputed to presumption and vainglory and will merit no reward. Therefore, let everything be done with the Abbot's approval. (Chapter 49, Part 1)

1 Thessalonians 1

[2] We always give thanks to God for all of you and mention you in our prayers, constantly [3] remembering before our God and Father your work of faith and labor of love and steadfastness of hope in our Lord Jesus Christ. [4] For we know, brothers and sisters beloved by God, that he has chosen you, [5] because our message of the

gospel came to you not in word only, but also in power and in the Holy Spirit and with full conviction; just as you know what kind of persons we proved to be among you for your sake. ⁶ And you became imitators of us and of the Lord, for in spite of persecution you received the word with joy inspired by the Holy Spirit, ⁷ so that you became an example to all the believers in Macedonia and in Achaia.

Contemplation

1. What word, phrase, or image from either of the two passages resonates with you?
2. What connection can you make to your own life?
3. What might God be calling you to do?

Reflection

What should I give up for Lent? Benedict makes the point that all of our life should manifest the abstinence and restraint of a Lenten observance. Isn't restraining ourselves from vice and giving ourselves to prayer, reading, and compunction of heart a good thing to practice year-round? What is the point of giving up chocolate, as a token sacrifice, intending that we will take it up again the minute Lent is over? What is the point of giving up chocolate while still being lax in our habits of prayer and study and service to others?

Benedict suggests that during Lent we increase the "usual burden of our service," perhaps by praying more faithfully or volunteering for that ministry we have felt called to join, as well as restraining ourselves from food and drink we don't need with greater intention. He further says we should do this of our own will, offering it to God with the "joy of the Holy Spirit." In other words, Lent should be joyfully observed. We don't do this to earn points with God, but rather out of deep gratitude for God's grace to us.

My intention this Lent is to give up indulgences that waste time and to more intentionally incorporate prayer, reading, exercise, music, and family into my daily routines because they bring me joy. And I hope that these always will be part of my Lenten life year-round.

Prayer

Gracious God, thank you for the joy of your Holy Spirit and the grace that inspires me to be intentional about all the things that are good for me and bring joy to others. Amen.

6

HUMILITY

HUMBLING MYSELF

From the Rule

Holy Scripture, brethren, cries out to us, saying, "Everyone who exalts himself shall be humbled, and he who humbles himself shall be exalted" (Luke 14:11). In saying this it shows us that all exaltation is a kind of pride, against which the Prophet proves himself to be on guard when he says, "Lord, my heart is not exalted, nor are mine eyes lifted up; neither have I walked in great matters, nor in wonders above me" (Ps. 131:1) But how has he acted? "Rather have I been of humble mind than exalting myself; as a weaned child on its mother's breast, so You solace my soul" (Ps. 131:2).

Hence, brethren, if we wish to reach the very highest point of humility and to arrive speedily at that heavenly exaltation to which ascent is made through the humility of this present life, we must by our ascending actions erect the ladder Jacob saw in his dream, on which Angels appeared to him descending and ascending. By that descent and ascent we must surely understand nothing else than this, that we descend by self-exaltation and ascend by humility. And the ladder thus set up is our life in the world, which the Lord raises up to heaven if our heart is humbled. For we call our body and soul the sides of the ladder, and into these sides our divine vocation has inserted the different steps of humility and discipline we must climb. (Chapter 7, Part 1)

Luke 14

[7] When he noticed how the guests chose the places of honor, he told them a parable. [8] "When you are invited by someone to a wedding banquet, do not sit down at the place of honor, in case someone more distinguished than you has been invited by your host; [9] and the host who invited both of you may come and say to you, 'Give this person your place,' and then in disgrace you would start to

take the lowest place. [10] But when you are invited, go and sit down at the lowest place, so that when your host comes, he may say to you, 'Friend, move up higher'; then you will be honored in the presence of all who sit at the table with you. [11] For all who exalt themselves will be humbled, and those who humble themselves will be exalted."

Contemplation

1. What word, phrase, or image from either of the two passages resonates with you?
2. What connection can you make to your own life?
3. What might God be calling you to do?

Reflection

We live in a culture that values appearance and achievement. However, I've known extremely talented artists, musicians, and scholars whom the world will never know, which has led me to the realization that to be widely recognized for what you do requires, in addition to talent and intelligence, incredible drive and a gift for self-promotion. The predominant culture reveres these proud, ambitious people. Against this context, Benedict echoes Jesus's words that to arrive at heavenly exaltation we must humble ourselves.

Esther de Waal writes about the contradictions in our life of faith.[1] We worship a God who becomes a man. As a victor he rides on a donkey in his hour of triumph. Our self-giving savior is executed like some common criminal. The first shall be last and the last shall be first. Much of our faith involves holding two seemingly contradictory truths in tension. To these we could add: "For all who exalt themselves will be humbled, and those who humble themselves will be exalted." The greatest paradox of faith is also something that Jesus said: "Those who lose their life for my sake will find it" (Matt. 10:39).

Prayer

Loving Jesus, who for our sake humbled yourself and became a servant, help me to understand that my worth is not in my earthly achievements. Help me to follow your example of humility and sacrifice. Amen.

---

1. Esther de Waal, *Living with Contradiction* (Harrisburg, PA: Morehouse, 1989), 155.

FEARING GOD

From the Rule

The first degree of humility, then, is that a person keep the fear of God before his eyes and beware of ever forgetting it. Let him be ever mindful of all that God has commanded; let his thoughts constantly recur to the hell-fire which will burn for their sins those who despise God, and to the life everlasting which is prepared for those who fear Him. Let him keep himself at every moment from sins and vices, whether of the mind, the tongue, the hands, the feet, or the self-will, and check also the desires of the flesh. (Chapter 7, Part 2)

Deuteronomy 10

[12] So now, O Israel, what does the LORD your God require of you? Only to fear the LORD your God, to walk in all his ways, to love him, to serve the LORD your God with all your heart and with all your soul, [13] and to keep the commandments of the LORD your God and his decrees that I am commanding you today, for your own well-being. . . .

[20] You shall fear the LORD your God; him alone you shall worship; to him you shall hold fast, and by his name you shall swear. [21] He is your praise; he is your God, who has done for you these great and awesome things that your own eyes have seen.

Contemplation

1. What word, phrase, or image from either of the two passages resonates with you?
2. What connection can you make to your own life?
3. What might God be calling you to do?

Reflection

Benedict's sixth-century concept of hell was a literal subterranean place of fire, where the unrepentant burned for their sins, and he equates fear of God to a fear of hell. However, the Bible usually frames the fear of God (or the fear of the Lord) in terms of appropriate reverence for a righteous judge who will bring justice, punishing those who oppress the downtrodden. Very often, images of God's awful wrath are followed by accounts of his love and benevolence.

Being humble begins with being respectful of God's power, keeping in check our own selfish and self-destructive impulses, and submitting to God in the activities of our mind, tongue, hands, feet, and self-will. We also will remember to praise the God "who has done for you these great and awesome things that your own eyes have seen."

Prayer

Almighty God, help me to be mindful of your power. Thank you for being the power for good in this world, and help me to submit my thoughts and being to your will. Amen.

CONSIDERING GOD

From the Rule

Let a man consider that God is always looking at him from heaven, that his actions are everywhere visible to the divine eyes and are constantly being reported to God by the Angels. This is what the Prophet shows us when he represents God as ever present within our thoughts, in the words "Searcher of minds and hearts is God" (Ps. 7:10) and again in the words "The Lord knows the thoughts of men" (Ps. 94:11). Again he says, "You have read my thoughts from afar" (Ps. 139:3) and "The thoughts of people will confess to You" (Ps. 76:11).

In order that he may be careful about his wrongful thoughts, therefore, let the faithful brother say constantly in his heart, "Then shall I be spotless before Him, if I have kept myself from my iniquity" (Ps. 18:24). (Chapter 7, Part 3)

Psalm 139

¹ O LORD, you have searched me and known me.
² You know when I sit down and when I rise up;
   you discern my thoughts from far away.
³ You search out my path and my lying down,
   and are acquainted with all my ways.
⁴ Even before a word is on my tongue,
   O LORD, you know it completely.
⁵ You hem me in, behind and before,
   and lay your hand upon me.
⁶ Such knowledge is too wonderful for me;
   it is so high that I cannot attain it.

Contemplation

1. What word, phrase, or image from either of the two passages resonates with you?
2. What connection can you make to your own life?
3. What might God be calling you to do?

Reflection

God is watching. Our omnipresent God is a "searcher of minds and hearts" and is acquainted with all our ways. Even before a word is on my tongue, God knows it completely. In the words of the Eucharist liturgy, "To you all hearts are open, all desires known, and from you no secrets are hid." This awareness should not be cause for anxiety or paranoia, but rather humility, keenly understanding that I can't fool God. My piety in front of friends and self-righteousness in front of enemies doesn't change what God knows about me.

The awareness of God's watchfulness should also be cause for comfort. God's presence means that I don't have to be anything else other than what I am. I can be nakedly honest in my prayers and I can tap into his wisdom about me and all my ways. I can trust the voice of the Holy Spirit. In the words of the psalm, "Such knowledge is too wonderful for me."

Prayer

Almighty God, to you all hearts are open, all desires known, and from you no secrets are hid. Help me never to pretend to be anything other than what I am and to live in the assurance of your knowledge of me and of what is best for me. Amen.

YIELDING MY SELF-WILL

From the Rule

As for self-will, we are forbidden to do our own will by the Scripture, which says to us, "Turn away from your own will" (Sir. 18:30), and likewise by the prayer in which we ask God that His will be done in us. And rightly are we taught not to do our own will when we take heed to the warning of Scripture: "There are ways which seem right, but the ends of them plunge into the depths of hell" (Prov. 16:25); and also when we tremble at what is said of the careless: "They are corrupt and have become abominable in their will."

And as for the desires of the flesh, let us believe with the Prophet that God is ever present to us, when he says to the Lord, "Every desire of mine is before You" (Ps. 38:10). (Chapter 7, Part 4)

Proverbs 16

18 Pride goes before destruction,
   and a haughty spirit before a fall.

¹⁹ It is better to be of a lowly spirit among the poor
   than to divide the spoil with the proud.
²⁰ Those who are attentive to a matter will prosper,
   and happy are those who trust in the LORD.
²¹ The wise of heart is called perceptive,
   and pleasant speech increases persuasiveness.
²² Wisdom is a fountain of life to one who has it,
   but folly is the punishment of fools.
²³ The mind of the wise makes their speech judicious,
   and adds persuasiveness to their lips.
²⁴ Pleasant words are like a honeycomb,
   sweetness to the soul and health to the body.
²⁵ Sometimes there is a way that seems to be right,
   but in the end it is the way to death.

Contemplation

1. What word, phrase, or image from either of the two passages resonates with you?
2. What connection can you make to your own life?
3. What might God be calling you to do?

Reflection

Our own will most often stands in the way of God's will. Proverbs 16 tells us that sometimes there is a way that seems to us to be right, "but in the end it is the way to death." Multiple examples come to mind: misguided foreign interventions, disastrous financial investments, and bad relationships are just a few.

Benedict is still addressing step one on the ladder of humility (keeping the fear of God before our eyes). He advises us to acknowledge God's sovereignty by turning away from our own will and praying that God will accomplish God's will in us. Probably the most difficult challenge for focused, self-disciplined, achievement-oriented people on their path to God's kingdom is giving up control of their own plans in order to take up our cross and follow Christ.

Prayer

Sovereign God, help me each day to yield my own will and selfish desires. Help me to see that following you, no matter how rocky the path and difficult the climb, is the way to eternal life. Amen.

SURRENDERING

From the Rule

The second degree of humility is that a person love not his own will nor take pleasure in satisfying his desires, but model his actions on the saying of the Lord, "I have come not to do My own will, but the will of Him who sent Me" (John 6:38). It is written also, "Self-will has its punishment, but constraint wins a crown." (Chapter 7, Part 6)

John 6

[35] Jesus said to them, "I am the bread of life. Whoever comes to me will never be hungry, and whoever believes in me will never be thirsty. [36] But I said to you that you have seen me and yet do not believe. [37] Everything that the Father gives me will come to me, and anyone who comes to me I will never drive away; [38] for I have come down from heaven, not to do my own will, but the will of him who sent me. [39] And this is the will of him who sent me, that I should lose nothing of all that he has given me, but raise it up on the last day. [40] This is indeed the will of my Father, that all who see the Son and believe in him may have eternal life; and I will raise them up on the last day."

Contemplation

1. What word, phrase, or image from either of the two passages resonates with you?
2. What connection can you make to your own life?
3. What might God be calling you to do?

Reflection

The second step of humility is to follow the words of Jesus and his example, surrendering our own will and pursuing the will of the one who placed us on earth. The hardest part of Benedict's advice for me is the part that says "nor take pleasure in satisfying his desires." I love to go out for expensive meals. I love many kinds of music. I love a nice wine and enjoy an occasional mixed drink. I have greatly enjoyed sex. How do I take no pleasure in these? I am a human with very human desires.

One response is to acknowledge the good things we enjoy as having come from God. There is nothing good that does not come from God. It is one thing to appreciate and—when appropriate—accommodate one's natural desires and another to live a life solely aimed at satisfying desire. Several years ago, I realized that satisfying desires, as enjoyable as that could be, was not enough for a rewarding life. I had a sudden awareness that I needed to go deeper in my faith. My prayer now is that I will realize more fully, day by day, the purpose God has for me, grow into God's love, and come to a place where God, and God alone, is enough.

Prayer

Merciful God, help me to realize more fully the purpose you have for me. Help me to love you and increasingly delight in the things of God until, one day, I will appreciate that you alone are enough. Amen.

SUBMITTING OURSELVES

From the Rule

The third degree of humility is that a person for love of God submit himself to his Superior in all obedience, imitating the Lord, of whom the Apostle says, "He became obedient even unto death." (Chapter 7, Part 7)

Philippians 2

If then there is any encouragement in Christ, any consolation from love, any sharing in the Spirit, any compassion and sympathy, [2] make my joy complete: be of the same mind, having the same love, being in full accord and of one mind. [3] Do nothing from selfish ambition or conceit, but in humility regard others as better than yourselves. [4] Let each of you look not to your own interests, but to the interests of others. [5] Let the same mind be in you that was in Christ Jesus,

> [6] who, though he was in the form of God,
> did not regard equality with God
> as something to be exploited,
> [7] but emptied himself,
> taking the form of a slave,
> being born in human likeness.
> And being found in human form,
> [8] he humbled himself
> and became obedient to the point of death—
> even death on a cross.

Contemplation

1. What word, phrase, or image from either of the two passages resonates with you?
2. What connection can you make to your own life?
3. What might God be calling you to do?

Reflection

Benedict explained in chapter 2 of the Rule that the abbot "is believed to hold the place of Christ in the monastery," and for this reason we are told to submit to our superior. It is not that the abbot is Christ, the source of our salvation, and certainly not as holy or sovereign as Christ. However, submitting to our superior is like a sacramental act in that it represents and honors our submission to Christ. As Benedict says, we do this "for love of God."

In our submission, we also understand that, according to the Rule, God holds abbots to an even higher standard. The abbot is accountable to God for those he or she oversees and must "show them all that is good and holy by his deeds even more than by his words." We can confidently submit to someone who, in turn, submits to God.

Prayer

Patient and loving God, help me show my love for you by honoring and submitting to those whom you have selected as my spiritual guides. Amen.

ENDURING WITH PATIENCE

From the Rule

The fourth degree of humility is that he hold fast to patience with a silent mind when in this obedience he meets with difficulties and contradictions and even any kind of injustice, enduring all without growing weary or running away. For the Scripture says, "The one who perseveres to the end, is the one who shall be saved" (Matt. 10:22); and again "Let your heart take courage, and wait for the Lord" (Ps. 27:14)!

And to show how those who are faithful ought to endure all things, however contrary, for the Lord, the Scripture says in the person of the suffering, "For Your sake we are put to death all the day long; we are considered as sheep marked for slaughter" (Ps. 44:22; Rom. 8:36). Then, secure in their hope of a divine recompense, they go on with joy to declare, "But in all these trials we conquer, through Him who has granted us His love" (Rom. 8:37). Again, in another place the

Scripture says, "You have tested us, O God; You have tried us as silver is tried, by fire; You have brought us into a snare; You have laid afflictions on our back" (Ps. 65[66]:10–11). And to show that we ought to be under a Superior, it goes on to say, "You have set men over our heads" (Ps. 66:12).

Moreover, by their patience those faithful ones fulfill the Lord's command in adversities and injuries: when struck on one cheek, they offer the other; when deprived of their tunic, they surrender also their cloak; when forced to go a mile, they go two; with the Apostle Paul they bear with false brethren (2 Cor. 11:26) and bless those who curse them (1 Cor. 4:12). (Chapter 7, Part 8)

Romans 8

[35] Who will separate us from the love of Christ? Will hardship, or distress, or persecution, or famine, or nakedness, or peril, or sword? [36] As it is written, "For your sake we are being killed all day long; we are accounted as sheep to be slaughtered." [37] No, in all these things we are more than conquerors through him who loved us. [38] For I am convinced that neither death, nor life, nor angels, nor rulers, nor things present, nor things to come, nor powers, [39] nor height, nor depth, nor anything else in all creation, will be able to separate us from the love of God in Christ Jesus our Lord.

Contemplation

1. What word, phrase, or image from either of the two passages resonates with you?
2. What connection can you make to your own life?
3. What might God be calling you to do?

Reflection

Hold fast. Persevere. Take courage. Wait on the Lord. Endure all things. With the help of scripture verses from the books of Romans, 1 and 2 Corinthians, and the Psalms, Benedict is saying that following Christ will not all be fun and games. The earliest Christians suffered great persecution, and during Benedict's time—after the fall of the Roman Empire and at the onset of the Middle Ages—Perugia was subject to barbarian attack, lacking strong defenses. But life couldn't have been easy inside the monastery either. Guided by *ora et labora*, there must have been lots of *labora* (physical work) in a self-sustaining community.

So where does humility come into all of this? Humility is found in "holding fast to patience *with a silent mind*." In other words, patiently doing one's work and obediently following direction without murmuring, silently cursing the abbot, questioning God, or getting angry at the brother who, because of indolence or indifference, creates more work for you. Submission in one's behavior is one thing; submission of one's mind is something else entirely.

Benedict has given a tall order here. I know that I will fall down and get up again many times on this one. Our comfort and encouragement come from knowing, as Paul said, that any kind of hardship or distress will not separate us from the love of God. In all things we can be "more than conquerors."

Prayer

Patient and merciful God, quiet my mind and quiet my spirit as I work today. Help me to bear whatever trouble or distress comes my way with humility, knowing that nothing will separate me from your love. Amen.

CONFESSING OUR SIN

From the Rule

The fifth degree of humility is that he hide from his Abbot none of the evil thoughts that enter his heart or the sins committed in secret, but that he humbly confess them. The Scripture urges us to this when it says, "Reveal your way to the Lord and hope in Him" (Ps. 37:5) and again, "Confess to the Lord, for He is good, for His mercy endures forever" (Ps. 106:1). And the Prophet likewise says, "My offense I have made known to You, and my iniquities I have not covered up. I said: 'I will declare against myself my iniquities to the Lord;' and 'You forgave the wickedness of my heart'" (Ps. 32:5). (Chapter 7, Part 9)

Psalm 32

1 Happy are those whose transgression is forgiven,
   whose sin is covered.
2 Happy are those to whom the LORD imputes no iniquity,
   and in whose spirit there is no deceit.
3 While I kept silence, my body wasted away
   through my groaning all day long.
4 For day and night your hand was heavy upon me;
   my strength was dried up as by the heat of summer. *Selah*
5 Then I acknowledged my sin to you,
   and I did not hide my iniquity;
   I said, "I will confess my transgressions to the LORD,"
   and you forgave the guilt of my sin. *Selah*

Contemplation

1. What word, phrase, or image from either of the two passages resonates with you?
2. What connection can you make to your own life?
3. What might God be calling you to do?

Reflection

I think most Christians are uncomfortable with the idea of confession to anyone but God. Episcopalians like to say they make confession every week (with everyone else in their pew in the liturgy of the Eucharist). However, several authors have underscored the value of having a spiritual guide or friend with whom we can share everything about our lives, even the parts of which we are ashamed and the temptations we struggle with. Naming a problem or challenge is most often the first step in being prepared to address it.

Many progressives have a hard time with the biblical notion of sin, but that has always mystified me. When I look around in the world, it isn't difficult to see brokenness and human failing. When I look at my own life, I certainly have regrets about hurtful things I've said or selfish things I've done.

It takes humility to confess these things to another. Benedict says that the abbot (a spiritual leader who represents Christ in the community) is the appropriate person with whom to share these confessions.

Prayer

Merciful God, forgive me for my inclination to hide my faults. Give me the courage to confess my sins and receive the comfort of your forgiveness. Amen.

BEING CONTENT

From the Rule

The sixth degree of humility is that a monk be content with the poorest and worst of everything, and that in every occupation assigned him he consider himself a bad and worthless workman, saying with the Prophet, "I am brought to nothing and I am without understanding; I have become as a beast of burden before You, and I am always with You" (Ps. 73:22–23). (Chapter 7, Part 10)

Psalm 73

21 When my soul was embittered,
   when I was pricked in heart,
22 I was stupid and ignorant;
   I was like a brute beast toward you.
23 Nevertheless I am continually with you;
   you hold my right hand.
24 You guide me with your counsel,
   and afterward you will receive me with honor.
25 Whom have I in heaven but you?
   And there is nothing on earth that I desire other than you.
26 My flesh and my heart may fail,
   but God is the strength of my heart and my portion forever.

Contemplation

1. What word, phrase, or image from either of the two passages resonates with you?
2. What connection can you make to your own life?
3. What might God be calling you to do?

Reflection

Benedict's sixth degree of humility is being content with what we are given, even if it is the poorest of choices in our own mind. We must keep in mind that the context in which Benedict writes this rule is a monastic community in which everyone is given clothes to wear, a bed to sleep on, plenty of food, and brothers who look after each other's needs. We cannot say to the homeless, food-insecure, or oppressed, "Be content with what you are given." Christ's teaching to love our neighbors as ourselves means that we cannot dismiss the dissatisfaction of others who struggle to meet even their basic needs.

However, for the majority of us who have enough, the quintessential twenty-first-century sin must be materialism. We live in a rampant consumerist society. After all, we have worked hard and come from the right kind of family. Shouldn't we have the kind of life, kind of clothes, kind of home we see that others have? We do not consider ourselves a "worthless workman." The poorest of choices won't do. Aren't we entitled to more?

The problem is that we are all culture-bound. It's hard for us to reject materialism when we see that the people with status around us wear nice clothes and have nice things. Benedict, following Christ's teaching, tells us that these things don't matter and that our happiness should come from our relationship to God. Humility requires taking this teaching to heart and saying with the psalmist, "There is nothing on earth that I desire other than you."

Prayer

Gracious and generous God, you have given me all that I need. Forgive me when, out of pride, I want more than I need. Help me be content with all that I have. Amen.

SELF-APPRAISAL

From the Rule

The seventh degree of humility is that he consider himself lower and of less account than anyone else, and this not only in verbal protestation but also with the most heartfelt inner conviction, humbling himself and saying with the Prophet, "But I am a worm and no man, the scorn of men and the outcast of the people" (Ps. 22:6). "After being exalted, I have been humbled and covered with confusion" (Ps. 88:16). And again, "It is good for me that You have humbled me, that I may learn Your commandments" (Ps. 119:71, 73). (Chapter 7, Part 11)

Luke 18

[9] He also told this parable to some who trusted in themselves that they were righteous and regarded others with contempt: [10] "Two men went up to the temple to pray, one a Pharisee and the other a tax collector. [11] The Pharisee, standing by himself, was praying thus, 'God, I thank you that I am not like other people: thieves, rogues, adulterers, or even like this tax collector. [12] I fast twice a week; I give a tenth of all my income.' [13] But the tax collector, standing far off, would not even look up to heaven, but was beating his breast and saying, 'God, be merciful to me, a sinner!' [14] I tell you, this man went down to his home justified rather than the other; for all who exalt themselves will be humbled, but all who humble themselves will be exalted."

Contemplation

1. What word, phrase, or image from either of the two passages resonates with you?
2. What connection can you make to your own life?
3. What might God be calling you to do?

Reflection

Even though Benedict did not cite the Luke 18 passage above when talking about how we should consider ourselves, it is the parable that comes to mind when I think about humility.

Volunteering every week in a program that provides hot meals to community members has helped me adjust my attitude toward others. Many of the people I have served are people I previously would have avoided if I saw them on the street. It is too easy for me think of myself as more favored in God's eyes because of my education, achievements, and comfortable life. "God, I thank you that I am not like other people." However, when I hear many of their stories, I also realize how much accident of birth and circumstances of chance are the reasons for our differences in situation. When I see their kindnesses toward others, their humility when talking about matters of faith, and their gratitude for what they have received, I realize that I have no basis for thinking that I have a more privileged status in God's eyes.

Not to say that I am never judgmental; I still have much to learn in this regard.

Prayer

Loving God, thank you for bringing into my life people who remind me of my own need for you. Continue to remind me that there is no one whom you do not love and of my own unworthiness of your grace. Amen.

HONORING THE RULE

From the Rule

The eighth degree of humility is that a monk do nothing except what is commended by the common rule of the monastery and the example of the elders. (Chapter 7, Part 12)

1 Corinthians 10

⁶ Now these things occurred as examples for us, so that we might not desire evil as they did. ⁷ Do not become idolaters as some of them did; as it is written, "The people sat down to eat and drink, and they rose up to play." ⁸ We must not indulge in sexual immorality as some of them did, and twenty-three thousand fell in a single day. ⁹ We must not put Christ to the test, as some of them did, and were destroyed by serpents. ¹⁰ And do not complain as some of them did, and were destroyed by

the destroyer. [11] These things happened to them to serve as an example, and they were written down to instruct us, on whom the ends of the ages have come. [12] So if you think you are standing, watch out that you do not fall. [13] No testing has overtaken you that is not common to everyone. God is faithful, and he will not let you be tested beyond your strength, but with the testing he will also provide the way out so that you may be able to endure it.

Contemplation

1. What word, phrase, or image from either of the two passages resonates with you?
2. What connection can you make to your own life?
3. What might God be calling you to do?

Reflection

Humility requires that we subjugate our own free will to the needs of the community. When you are a member of a community, you do not have the freedom to live by your own rules. People who live together must come to a common understanding about how they will live their life together. You must follow the rules of the group for the sake of community harmony. In the case of a Benedictine community, we follow the Rule of Benedict. Benedict adds here that, when there isn't a stated guideline in the Rule, we follow the example of the spiritual elders within our fellowship.

We are to assume the role of a learner or apprentice. The apostle Paul cautions that we must not be complacent in the way we do this. "If you think you are standing, watch out that you do not fall." The great comfort, of course, is that we serve a loving God who will always provide us the grace to endure.

Prayer

Patient God, help me to hold in check my inclination to follow my own rules and desires. Help me to look to you and to the example of those who have gone before me on the path to eternal life. Amen.

Restraining the Tongue

From the Rule

The ninth degree of humility is that a monk restrain his tongue and keep silence, not speaking until he is questioned. For the Scripture shows that "in much speaking there is no escape from sin" (Prov. 10:19) and that "the talkative man is not stable on the earth" (Ps. 140:11). (Chapter 7, Part 13)

Proverbs 10

¹⁷ Whoever heeds instruction is on the path to life,
   but one who rejects a rebuke goes astray.
¹⁸ Lying lips conceal hatred,
   and whoever utters slander is a fool.
¹⁹ When words are many, transgression is not lacking,
   but the prudent are restrained in speech.
²⁰ The tongue of the righteous is choice silver;
   the mind of the wicked is of little worth.
²¹ The lips of the righteous feed many,
   but fools die for lack of sense.

Contemplation

1. What word, phrase, or image from either of the two passages resonates with you?
2. What connection can you make to your own life?
3. What might God be calling you to do?

Reflection

Restraint of speech is one of the signature disciplines of Benedictines. We all have something to say and we want our voice to be heard. However, out of humility, we must suppress the impulse to always be heard.

Why? First, restraint of speech is essential to attentive listening. I have often caught myself in conversations not really listening to what others are saying because I am thinking about what I am anxiously waiting to say next. Although we may think about the point we want to make, we often don't give serious thought to its appropriateness and what it adds to the discussion. And then there are the thoughtless words, the things we wish we could take back after we've said them. The Proverb states, "When words are many, transgression is not lacking," or as Benedict puts it, "In much speaking there is no escape from sin."

Prayer

Patient and loving God, give me the humility to be a thoughtful listener, realizing that my own speech isn't the most important voice in the room. Help me also to realize the damage that thoughtless words can do. Amen.

Restraining Our Humor

From the Rule

The tenth degree of humility is that he be not ready and quick to laugh, for it is written, "The fool lifts up his voice in laughter" (Sir. 21:20). (Chapter 7, Part 14)

Sirach 21

15 When an intelligent person hears a wise saying,
   he praises it and adds to it;
   when a fool hears it, he laughs at it
   and throws it behind his back.
16 A fool's chatter is like a burden on a journey,
   but delight is found in the speech of the intelligent.
17 The utterance of a sensible person is sought in the assembly,
   and they ponder his words in their minds.
18 Like a house in ruins is wisdom to a fool,
   and to the ignorant, knowledge is talk that has no meaning.
19 To a senseless person education is fetters on his feet,
   and like manacles on his right hand.
20 A fool raises his voice when he laughs,
   but the wise smile quietly.

Contemplation

1. What word, phrase, or image from either of the two passages resonates with you?
2. What connection can you make to your own life?
3. What might God be calling you to do?

Reflection

Another translation of the word "fool" in the passage that Benedict cites is "reveler." It is clear from the Sirach reference that the reveler Benedict is writing about is dismissive ("he laughs at it and throws it behind his back") and loud ("raises his voice").

Benedictines are not humorless. A visit to almost any monastery would put that idea to rest. I think Benedict is making a case for respectful humor that is not at the expense of others, does not belittle wisdom, and does not draw attention to itself. One wonders what may have passed for humor in sixth-century Italy.

Certainly, in our own age, we've experienced profane humor and loud humor that sabotages serious conversation.

Benedict is making the point that restraining our use of humor is an act of humility. This attitude certainly does not preclude taking delight in people and seeing the humor in the amusing things that happen in everyday life.

Prayer

God, who created us in your own image, thank you for the world around us and the things you have made that delight us. Give me a humble sense of humor that does not call attention to myself or belittle those around me. Amen.

SPEAKING GENTLY

From the Rule

The eleventh degree of humility is that when a monk speaks he do so gently and without laughter, humbly and seriously, in few and sensible words, and that he be not noisy in his speech. It is written, "A wise man is known by the fewness of his words" (Sextus, *Enchidirion*, 134 or 145). (Chapter 7, Part 15)

Deuteronomy 32

1 Give ear, O heavens, and I will speak;
   let the earth hear the words of my mouth.
2 May my teaching drop like the rain,
   my speech condense like the dew;
   like gentle rain on grass,
   like showers on new growth.
3 For I will proclaim the name of the LORD;
   ascribe greatness to our God!

Contemplation

1. What word, phrase, or image from either of the two passages resonates with you?
2. What connection can you make to your own life?
3. What might God be calling you to do?

Reflection

The Deuteronomy passage is a song that Moses recited at the end of his life, in the hearing of the whole assembly of Israel. "May . . . my speech condense like the dew, like gentle rain on grass." In other words, may my speech be gentle and concise, refreshing those who listen.

However, it is interesting that Benedict does not quote scripture in this section of the Rule. The *enchidirion* that Benedict cites here is a handbook of Roman law by Sextus Pomponius, a second-century jurist. Economy of speech was something that was valued by secular leaders as well as religious.

Being around those who talk too much can be difficult. It is sometimes emotionally exhausting. How much I appreciate friends who have a gentle presence. They don't need to say much, and when they do, their words refresh like the dew.

Prayer

Gentle Savior, give me a gentleness of spirit that is a calming presence to those around me. Give me words that refresh and not irritate, that heal and not hurt. Amen.

ACKNOWLEDGING OUR SINFULNESS

From the Rule

The twelfth degree of humility is that a monk not only have humility in his heart but also by his very appearance make it always manifest to those who see him. That is to say that whether he is at the Work of God, in the oratory, in the monastery, in the garden, on the road, in the fields or anywhere else, and whether sitting, walking, or standing, he should always have his head bowed and his eyes toward the ground. Feeling the guilt of his sins at every moment, he should consider himself already present at the dread Judgment and constantly say in his heart what the publican in the Gospel said with his eyes fixed on the earth: "Lord, I am a sinner and not worthy to lift up my eyes to heaven" (Luke 18:13; Matt. 8:8); and again with the Prophet: "I am bowed down and humbled everywhere" (Ps. 38:7, 9; 119:107).

Having climbed all these steps of humility, therefore, the monk will presently come to that perfect love of God which casts out fear. And all those precepts which formerly he had not observed without fear, he will now begin to keep by reason of that love, without any effort, as though naturally and by habit. No longer will his motive be the fear of hell, but rather the love of Christ, good habit and delight in the virtues which the Lord will deign to show forth by the Holy Spirit in His servant now cleansed from vice and sin. (Chapter 7, Part 16)

Luke 18

[9] He also told this parable to some who trusted in themselves that they were righteous and regarded others with contempt: [10] "Two men went up to the temple to pray, one a Pharisee and the other a tax collector. [11] The Pharisee, standing by himself, was praying thus, 'God, I thank you that I am not like other people: thieves, rogues, adulterers, or even like this tax collector. [12] I fast twice a week; I give a tenth of all my income.' [13] But the tax collector, standing far off, would not even look up to heaven, but was beating his breast and saying, 'God, be merciful to me, a sinner!' [14] I tell you, this man went down to his home justified rather than the other; for all who exalt themselves will be humbled, but all who humble themselves will be exalted."

Contemplation

1. What word, phrase, or image from either of the two passages resonates with you?
2. What connection can you make to your own life?
3. What might God be calling you to do?

Reflection

The final step of humility is acknowledging, before all, our imperfections and sinfulness. Self-righteous pride has no place in following Christ. Revealing all that we genuinely are, or what Ian Morgan Cron referred to as "the radically unprotected life,"[2] is our calling as Christians. This transparency is difficult for one who was raised to demonstrate his piety and best behavior when in church and around church people. Growing up, I would never imagine confessing my spiritual struggles to my church friends. It was our shining victories that we shared.

The more we understand and acknowledge our true selves, the kinder and less judgmental we will be with others. We are all in the same boat—dependent on God's forgiveness and grace.

Benedict concludes by saying that being able to look at ourselves humbly, without exaggerated pride or self-flagellating judgment, brings us to what should be the true motivation for our spiritual journey—not fear of hell, but love for

---

2. Ian Morgan Cron, *Chasing Francis* (Grand Rapids, MI: Zondervan, 2006), 71.

God. I love these words from the General Thanksgiving in the Book of Common Prayer (Rite Two, Morning and Evening Prayer): "Give us such an awareness of your mercies, that with truly thankful hearts we may show forth your praise, not only with our lips, but in our lives. . . ."

Prayer

Merciful God, thank you for accepting me and loving me as I truly am. Help me to always be honest in presenting myself to others as I really am. Amen.

FOLLOWING JESUS'S EXAMPLE

From the Rule

If it happens that difficult or impossible tasks are laid on a brother, let him nevertheless receive the order of the one in authority with all meekness and obedience. But if he sees that the weight of the burden altogether exceeds the limit of his strength, let him submit the reasons for his inability to the one who is over him in a quiet way and at an opportune time, without pride, resistance, or contradiction. And if after these representations the Superior still persists in his decision and command, let the subject know that this is for his good, and let him obey out of love, trusting in the help of God. (Chapter 68)

Philippians 2

[5] Let the same mind be in you that was in Christ Jesus, [6] who, though he was in the form of God, did not regard equality with God as something to be exploited, [7] but emptied himself, taking the form of a slave, being born in human likeness. And being found in human form, [8] he humbled himself and became obedient to the point of death—even death on a cross. [9] Therefore God also highly exalted him and gave him the name that is above every name, [10] so that at the name of Jesus every knee should bend, in heaven and on earth and under the earth, [11] and every tongue should confess that Jesus Christ is Lord, to the glory of God the Father.

[12] Therefore, my beloved, just as you have always obeyed me, not only in my presence, but much more now in my absence, work out your own salvation with fear and trembling; [13] for it is God who is at work in you, enabling you both to will and to work for his good pleasure. [14] Do all things without murmuring and arguing, [15] so that you may be blameless and innocent, children of God without blemish in the midst of a crooked and perverse generation, in which you shine like stars in the world.

Contemplation

1. What word, phrase, or image from either of the two passages resonates with you?
2. What connection can you make to your own life?
3. What might God be calling you to do?

Reflection

In just about everyone's work life, one is asked by the boss to do the nearly impossible: have the entire area swept and mopped in half an hour, have the report on my desk by six o'clock tonight, cut your budget by 10 percent. According to Benedict, this happens in the monastery as well. A monk might be asked to spend hours in back-breaking labor in the fields, or care for a sick and somewhat senile elder, or take charge of preparing a large meal for the first time. (For some, the impossible will look like getting up at three thirty in the morning to pray the office of Vigils.)

The seemingly impossible challenge in my life was interacting with street people, the kind who are poorly dressed, foul-mouthed, and often don't smell too good. The kind I worked to avoid on the street. One Sunday, my priest talked about the church's food ministry and offered an invitation to the congregation to "come have lunch with us on Wednesday." I immediately said to myself, *No thank you.* I also immediately realized it was not the reaction Jesus would have and might be something I needed to examine. So, the following week I showed up on Wednesday, and was greeted at the door and directed to a table with five other men. I was very nervous about this, wondering what I would say to men that I had nothing in common with. Surprisingly, the conversation was free-flowing and pleasant. Upon leaving, I knew that I needed to come back as a volunteer, and that's what I did.

I learned that it isn't hard to see the Christ in others once you get to know them. Spending time with the church's neighbors opened my heart in ways that I never thought possible. Moreover, I learned that God honors us when we take risks to practice our faith. Even the most menial tasks become deeply gratifying and sacred work.

When a supervisor does not seem sympathetic to our complaints and directs us back to the work we really don't want to do, it may be to teach us these very lessons. It may be that attempting the impossible is the only way to find out how far one can go with God's help.

Prayer

God of wisdom, be patient with my resistance and reluctance to do your work. Teach me obedience to your will and open my heart to those you are calling me to serve. Amen.

7

∼

LEADERSHIP

The One Who Chooses

From the Rule

In the constituting of an Abbot let this plan always be followed, that the office be conferred on the one who is chosen either by the whole community unanimously in the fear of God or else by a part of the community, however small, if its counsel is more wholesome.

Merit of life and wisdom of doctrine should determine the choice of the one to be constituted, even if he be the last in the order of the community.

But if (which God forbid) the whole community should agree to choose a person who will acquiesce in their vices, and if those vices somehow become known to the Bishop to whose diocese the place belongs, or to the Abbots or the faithful of the vicinity, let them prevent the success of this conspiracy of the wicked, and set a worthy steward over the house of God. They may be sure that they will receive a good reward for this action if they do it with a pure intention and out of zeal for God; as, on the contrary, they will sin if they fail to do it. (Chapter 64, Part 1)

John 15

[12] This is my commandment, that you love one another as I have loved you. [13] No one has greater love than this, to lay down one's life for one's friends. [14] You are my friends if you do what I command you. [15] I do not call you servants any longer, because the servant does not know what the master is doing; but I have called you friends, because I have made known to you everything that I have heard from my Father. [16] You did not choose me but I chose you. And I appointed you to go and bear fruit, fruit that will last, so that the Father will give you whatever you ask him in my name. [17] I am giving you these commands so that you may love one another.

Contemplation

1. What word, phrase, or image from either of the two passages resonates with you?
2. What connection can you make to your own life?
3. What might God be calling you to do?

Reflection

The word "abbot" is a variation of the word *abba* (Aramaic for "father") and speaks to the parental nature taken on by the leader of the community. There are many with leadership abilities that don't necessarily have the qualities of a nurturing parent. Benedict goes on to say the abbot should be one who is a teacher and a shepherd, gently bringing back to the fold individuals who are disobedient to the Rule or groups who lose sight of their purpose. The abbot shepherds the community through prayerful listening, counseling, and direction.

According to Benedict, the guiding principle for choosing an abbot is that he or she should be someone either (a) selected by the whole community unanimously or (b) chosen by a part of the community, "no matter how small, which possesses sounder judgment." It appears that Benedict knew that not all groups could come to a consensus or use sound judgment in making a decision; therefore, the (b) option: a smaller group that has sounder judgment.

However, another factor is not mentioned in this chapter of the Rule; that it is the Holy Spirit who is the one who calls the leader of the community and moves the hearts of those who ostensibly do the choosing. As Jesus reminds his disciples in the Gospel of John, "You did not choose me but I chose you. And I appointed you to go and bear fruit."

Prayer

Loving Father who, in your wisdom, calls those who are chosen to be spiritual leaders, keep us all sensitive to your call and remind us to honor those who have obeyed your call to lead, teach, and shepherd. Amen.

THE IDEAL LEADER

From the Rule

Once he has been constituted, let the Abbot always bear in mind what a burden he has undertaken and to whom he will have to give an account of his stewardship, and let him know that his duty is rather to profit his brethren than to preside over them. He must therefore be learned in the divine law, that he may have a treasure of knowledge from which to bring forth new things and old. He must be chaste, sober, and merciful. Let him exalt mercy above judgment, that he himself may obtain mercy. He should hate vices; he should love the brethren.

In administering correction he should act prudently and not go to excess, lest in seeking too eagerly to scrape off the rust he break the vessel. Let him keep his own frailty ever before his eyes and remember that the bruised reed must not be broken. By this we do not mean that he should allow vices to grow; on the contrary, as we have already said, he should eradicate them prudently and with charity, in the way which may seem best in each case. Let him study rather to be loved than to be feared.

Let him not be excitable and worried, nor exacting and headstrong, nor jealous and over-suspicious; for then he is never at rest.

In his commands let him be prudent and considerate; and whether the work which he enjoins concerns God or the world, let him be discreet and moderate, bearing in mind the discretion of holy Jacob, who said, "If I cause my flocks to be overdriven, they will all die in one day" (Gen. 33:13). Taking this, then, and other examples of discretion, the mother of virtues, let him so temper all things that the strong may have something to strive after, and the weak may not fall back in dismay.

And especially let him keep this Rule in all its details, so that after a good ministry he may hear from the Lord what the good servant heard who gave his fellow-servants wheat in due season: "Indeed, I tell you, he will set him over all his goods" (Matt. 24:47). (Chapter 64, Part 2)

Genesis 33

[12] Then Esau said, "Let us journey on our way, and I will go alongside you." [13] But Jacob said to him, "My lord knows that the children are frail and that the flocks and herds, which are nursing, are a care to me; and if they are overdriven for one day, all the flocks will die. [14] Let my lord pass on ahead of his servant, and I will lead on slowly, according to the pace of the cattle that are before me and according to the pace of the children, until I come to my lord in Seir."

Contemplation

1. What word, phrase, or image from either of the two passages resonates with you?
2. What connection can you make to your own life?
3. What might God be calling you to do?

Reflection

As a new leader in my college at a large urban university, I remember a day, at the beginning of term, when a temperamental associate professor called the dean's office and bitterly complained about the room he'd been assigned for one of his classes (the biggest classroom in the building). He was angry that there were insufficient tables and chairs in the room to accommodate all the students in his large class and made it clear that it was not his job to make it right. I relayed that to my dean, thinking he, like me, would be annoyed by the manner in which the faculty member informed us of the problem. Instead, the dean simply smiled and said, "How long do you think it would take us to bring a couple of tables and a few chairs into the room?" We quickly located the necessary seating in rooms that had extra and carried them into the instructor's classroom. It took us less than ten minutes. As we left the room, the dean said to me, "That's servant leadership." I called the faculty member to say that the matter had been taken care of and realized I had learned a valuable lesson.

When choosing an abbot, Benedict recommends a truly extraordinary person. In identifying the qualities of a good abbot, his words represent the balance and moderation reflected throughout the Rule. An ideal leader, above all, should not be authoritarian. His duty is to profit his brethren rather than to preside over them, choosing mercy above judgment, and not being excessive in his correction. He (or she) should be like Jacob, in the Genesis account, sensitive to those who are stressed, exhausted, or too frail to keep up. He should be knowledgeable in spiritual matters and humble, keeping "his own frailty ever before his eyes." And most importantly, he should love the brethren. A good leader acts from a place of love, not judgment.

Prayer

Patient and wise God, teach me your patience, wisdom, and mercy. In my opportunities to lead, help me be a servant to all. Amen.

LEADING

From the Rule

An Abbot who is worthy to be over a monastery should always remember what he is called and live up to the name of Superior. For he is believed to hold the place of Christ in the monastery, being called by a name of His, which is taken from the words of the Apostle: "You have received a Spirit of adoption . . . , by virtue of which we cry, 'Abba—Father'" (Rom. 8:15)! Therefore, the Abbot ought not to teach or ordain or command anything which is against the Lord's precepts; on the contrary, his commands and his teaching should be a leaven of divine justice kneaded into the minds of his disciples. (Chapter 2, Part 1)

Romans 8

[12] So then, brothers and sisters, we are debtors, not to the flesh, to live according to the flesh— [13] for if you live according to the flesh, you will die; but if by the Spirit you put to death the deeds of the body, you will live. [14] For all who are led by the Spirit of God are children of God. [15] For you did not receive a spirit of slavery to fall back into fear, but you have received a spirit of adoption. When we cry, "Abba! Father!" [16] it is that very Spirit bearing witness with our spirit that we are children of God, [17] and if children, then heirs, heirs of God and joint heirs with Christ—if, in fact, we suffer with him so that we may also be glorified with him.

Contemplation

1. What word, phrase, or image from either of the two passages resonates with you?
2. What connection can you make to your own life?
3. What might God be calling you to do?

Reflection

Essential to any functioning community is a capable leader. Benedict tells us the abbot represents Christ in the monastery.

In what ways would Christ be the model for spiritual leaders to follow? Jesus loved his followers, especially the weakest, most disreputable, and most vulnerable among them. He reached out to tax collectors, adulterers, lepers, and others marginalized by the larger community. His life was devoted to ministering to others. He was a teacher who, among other things, taught his disciples to pray. Jesus himself spent hours in prayer. He challenged those who were self-righteous or complacent but was welcoming and forgiving to the repentant.

Of course, no spiritual leader, being human, can live up to Christ's perfect example, and we must forgive and support our leaders when they are human. But the abbot's role is to remind us of Christ's own example, both in teaching "the Lord's precepts" and in living out the Gospel day to day.

Prayer

Loving God, who is present to us as a loving father and nurturing mother, I pray for the leaders of my religious community. Give them the courage and compassion to challenge the complacent, welcome the outcast, and nurture the weak. Amen.

SHEPHERDING

From the Rule

Let the Abbot always bear in mind that at the dread Judgment of God there will be an examination of these two matters: his teaching and the obedience of his disciples. And let the Abbot be sure that any lack of profit the master of the house may find in the sheep will be laid to the blame of the shepherd. On the other hand, if the shepherd has bestowed all his pastoral diligence on a restless, unruly flock and tried every remedy for their unhealthy behavior, then he will be acquitted at the Lord's Judgment and may say to the Lord with the Prophet: "I have not concealed Your justice within my heart; Your truth and Your salvation I have declared" (Ps. 40:11). "But they have despised and rejected me" (Isa. 1:2; Ezech. 20:27). And then finally let death itself, irresistible, punish those disobedient sheep under his charge. (Chapter 2, Part 2)

Psalm 40

⁸ "I delight to do your will, O my God;
   your law is within my heart."
⁹ I have told the glad news of deliverance
   in the great congregation;
   See, I have not restrained my lips,
   as you know, O LORD.
¹⁰ I have not hidden your saving help within my heart,
   I have spoken of your faithfulness and your salvation;
   I have not concealed your steadfast love and your faithfulness
   from the great congregation.

Contemplation

1. What word, phrase, or image from either of the two passages resonates with you?
2. What connection can you make to your own life?
3. What might God be calling you to do?

Reflection

Benedict likens the abbot to a shepherd. He (or she) is responsible for sound teaching, leading the flock along sure paths to an obedient and holy life. In ancient times, as today, the shepherd's duty was to keep the flock intact and safe. Jesus called himself the Good Shepherd. In his book *A Shepherd Looks at Psalm 23,*

Phillip Keller[1] wrote that a good shepherd is a careful manager who, from time to time, makes a careful assessment of each individual sheep. He runs his hands over the sheep's body and through its fleece, carefully examining the sheep to see if all is well and looking for any sign of trouble. Followers of Christ, like sheep, tend to do poorly at taking care of themselves, frequently putting themselves in the path of danger and occasionally getting lost. The abbot's responsibility is to lead diligently, teaching stability and obedience to an unruly flock.

Prayer

Faithful and caring God, be with those who lead your flock. Give them the wisdom and diligence needed to teach those who are sometimes willful and wandering followers. Help me to be obedient to your leading and listen attentively to those you have sent to shepherd. Amen.

TEACHING BY EXAMPLE

From the Rule

Therefore, when anyone receives the name of Abbot, he ought to govern his disciples with a twofold teaching. That is to say, he should show them all that is good and holy by his deeds even more than by his words, expounding the Lord's commandments in words to the intelligent among his disciples, but demonstrating the divine precepts by his actions for those of harder hearts and ruder minds. And whatever he has taught his disciples to be contrary to God's law, let him indicate by his example that it is not to be done, lest, while preaching to others, he himself be found reprobate (1 Cor. 9:27), and lest God one day say to him in his sin, "Why do you declare My statutes and profess My covenant with your lips, whereas you hate discipline and have cast My words behind you" (Ps. 50:16–17)? And again, "You were looking at the speck in your brother's eye, and did not see the beam in your own" (Matt. 7:3). (Chapter 2, Part 3)

Matthew 7

[1] Do not judge, so that you may not be judged. [2] For with the judgment you make you will be judged, and the measure you give will be the measure you get. [3] Why do you see the speck in your neighbor's eye, but do not notice the log in your own

---

1. W. Phillip Keller, *A Shepherd Looks at Psalm 23* (Grand Rapids, MI: Zondervan, 1974).

eye? [4] Or how can you say to your neighbor, "Let me take the speck out of your eye," while the log is in your own eye? [5] You hypocrite, first take the log out of your own eye, and then you will see clearly to take the speck out of your neighbor's eye.

Contemplation

1. What word, phrase, or image from either of the two passages resonates with you?
2. What connection can you make to your own life?
3. What might God be calling you to do?

Reflection

One of the most powerful things I learned as a young teacher was the value of providing a model. Teaching a new skill requires modeling the behavior you would like the student to emulate. Words are useful, for those who pay attention and can understand them, but even more powerful is seeing an example of the desired behavior. A model is critical for those who might not entirely understand a verbal explanation.

Benedict says that the abbot is a teacher. Abbots, like all leaders, will be judged by the extent to which their life has integrity or, in other words, the degree to which their behavior is consistent with their teaching. Abbots also should be careful that their life example excludes those things that are not to be imitated. Benedict points to Matthew 7 to make clear that leaders will be judged by the same standard they use to judge others.

Prayer

Faithful Shepherd, let my life be an example to others. Help me to be obedient, even as I encourage others to be obedient. Shine your light on those areas of my life where I am blind, that I may be a better example of your righteousness, love, and grace. Amen.

LOVING ALL

From the Rule

Let him [the Abbot] make no distinction of persons in the monastery. Let him not love one more than another, unless it be one whom he finds better in good works or in obedience. Let him not advance one of noble birth ahead of one who was formerly a slave, unless there be some other reasonable ground for it. But if the

Abbot for just reason think fit to do so, let him advance one of any rank whatever. Otherwise let them keep their due places; because, whether slaves or freemen, we are all one in Christ (Gal. 3:28) and bear an equal burden of service in the army of the same Lord. For with God there is no respect of persons (Rom. 2:11). Only for one reason are we preferred in His sight: if we be found better than others in good works and humility. Therefore let the Abbot show equal love to all and impose the same discipline on all according to their desserts. (Chapter 2, Part 4)

Romans 2

6 For he will repay according to each one's deeds: 7 to those who by patiently doing good seek for glory and honor and immortality, he will give eternal life; 8 while for those who are self-seeking and who obey not the truth but wickedness, there will be wrath and fury. 9 There will be anguish and distress for everyone who does evil, the Jew first and also the Greek, 10 but glory and honor and peace for everyone who does good, the Jew first and also the Greek. 11 For God shows no partiality.

Contemplation

1. What word, phrase, or image from either of the two passages resonates with you?
2. What connection can you make to your own life?
3. What might God be calling you to do?

Reflection

God shows no partiality; God loves every person. Similarly, spiritual leaders should love each person in their charge and show no favoritism. If we aspire to bearing the image of Christ, we should love each person with whom we interact, regardless of their wealth, attractiveness, or social standing.

This is our sacred aspiration. However, I know of no one who can honestly say they love all people equally. Most of us would admit that there are those whom we find extremely difficult to love, sometimes within our own family. There are two commands here: (a) to love each person, and (b) show no favoritism. Benedict seems to acknowledge implicitly that there will be some we tend to love more. He indicates this when he writes, "Let him not love one more than another, *unless* it be one whom he finds better in good works or in obedience." The real issue for a leader is showing favoritism, especially on the basis of privilege or social standing. Everyone should be treated with love. Benedict says, "make no distinction of persons." However, as taught in Romans 2, it is reasonable for leaders to honor merit, acknowledging and rewarding those who excel "in good works or in obedience."

The challenge here for followers of Christ is humility, "keeping their due places," in spite of what they think their rank or reward should be. As Benedict points out, we are all one in Christ. We all need to remember that (myself included) when we encounter the person in our church community who irritates the hell out of us.

Prayer

Loving Savior, teach me my place in the body of Christ. Give me the humility to appreciate your love as one of many whom Christ loves. And, like Christ, help me to love, without partiality, all whom you love. Amen.

WHAT I AM

From the Rule

The Abbot should always remember what he is and what he is called, and should know that to whom more is committed, from him more is required (Luke 12:48). Let him understand also what a difficult and arduous task he has undertaken: ruling souls and adapting himself to a variety of characters. One he must coax, another scold, another persuade, according to each one's character and understanding. Thus he must adjust and adapt himself to all in such a way that he may not only suffer no loss in the flock committed to his care, but may even rejoice in the increase of a good flock. (Chapter 2, Part 6)

Luke 12

[42] And the Lord said, "Who then is the faithful and prudent manager whom his master will put in charge of his slaves, to give them their allowance of food at the proper time? [43] Blessed is that slave whom his master will find at work when he arrives. [44] Truly I tell you, he will put that one in charge of all his possessions. [45] But if that slave says to himself, 'My master is delayed in coming,' and if he begins to beat the other slaves, men and women, and to eat and drink and get drunk, [46] the master of that slave will come on a day when he does not expect him and at an hour that he does not know, and will cut him in pieces, and put him with the unfaithful. [47] That slave who knew what his master wanted, but did not prepare himself or do what was wanted, will receive a severe beating. [48] But the one who did not know and did what deserved a beating will receive a light beating. From everyone to whom much has been given, much will be required; and from the one to whom much has been entrusted, even more will be demanded."

Contemplation

1. What word, phrase, or image from either of the two passages resonates with you?
2. What connection can you make to your own life?
3. What might God be calling you to do?

Reflection

It is interesting that the scripture Benedict cites does not refer to abbots or priests or even religious leaders in general. Jesus's words in the Luke passage refer to a slave who is put in charge of other slaves. In other words, the abbot, like the other monks, is a humble servant of his Master, but the Master's expectations for the one in charge are even greater. Both Benedict and the passage from Luke suggest that an abbot will be punished more severely for disobedience, because he has been entrusted with more. And with what has he been entrusted? The physical and spiritual well-being of the monks in his charge.

Benedict begins by saying that the abbot "should always remember what he is and what he is called." As he points out in the first section of the Rule's chapter on abbots, the word "abbot" is a variation of the word *abba* and is an intimate name for one's father. The abbot is also shepherd, teacher, and model, being the representation of Christ in the community.

We, too, must often remind ourselves what we are and to what we are called. I identify myself as a Christian, a follower of Jesus, although I am certainly an imperfect representation of Christ to my friends, family, and the communities to which I belong. My prayer is to grow into the image of Christ more each day.

Prayer

Loving Father, thank you for the remarkable gift and the awesome responsibility of being a follower of Jesus. Remind me each day what I am and to whom I belong. Help me to reflect your image. Amen.

WELFARE OF SOULS

From the Rule

Above all let him not neglect or undervalue the welfare of the souls committed to him, in a greater concern for fleeting, earthly, perishable things; but let him always bear in mind that he has undertaken the government of souls and that he will have to give an account of them.

And if he be tempted to allege a lack of earthly means, let him remember what is written: "First seek the kingdom of God and His justice, and all these things shall be given you besides" (Matt. 6:33). And again: "Nothing is wanting to those who fear Him" (Ps. 34:10).

Let him know, then, that he who has undertaken the government of souls must prepare himself to render an account of them. Whatever number of brethren he knows he has under his care, he may be sure beyond doubt that on Judgment Day he will have to give the Lord an account of all these souls, as well as of his own soul.

Thus the constant apprehension about his coming examination as shepherd (Ezek. 34) concerning the sheep entrusted to him, and his anxiety over the account that must be given for others, make him careful of his own record. And while by his admonitions he is helping others to amend, he himself is cleansed of his faults. (Chapter 2, Part 7)

Psalm 34

⁴ I sought the LORD, and he answered me,
   and delivered me from all my fears.
⁵ Look to him, and be radiant;
   so your faces shall never be ashamed.
⁶ This poor soul cried, and was heard by the LORD,
   and was saved from every trouble.
⁷ The angel of the LORD encamps
   around those who fear him, and delivers them.
⁸ O taste and see that the LORD is good;
   happy are those who take refuge in him.
⁹ O fear the LORD, you his holy ones,
   for those who fear him have no want.
¹⁰ The young lions suffer want and hunger,
   but those who seek the LORD lack no good thing.

Contemplation

1. What word, phrase, or image from either of the two passages resonates with you?
2. What connection can you make to your own life?
3. What might God be calling you to do?

Reflection

The dean of the graduate school in which I taught for several years referred to her department chairs as the "chief worriers." It was their job to worry over the health of their programs, the performance of their faculty, and the well-being of their students. In this passage from the Rule, Benedict acknowledges the weight of responsibility an abbot is under in his concern for the monks in his charge, the "souls committed to him." He uses the words "apprehension" and "anxiety" when describing the account that they must give to God.

However—and this is the wonderful part of this section—Benedict also reminds the reader of God's support to those who undertake "the government of souls." As in the previous section, he emphasizes accountability, but his message is also tempered with reminders of God's grace. Nothing will be wanting. God will supply the strength a leader needs. And with the responsibility, comes great reward. While guiding the spiritual formation of those in their charge, through admonitions and encouragement, spiritual leaders are themselves cleansed of faults. In other words, they are strengthened on their own spiritual journey. The abbot, being the representative of Christ in the monastery, is growing more fully into the image of Christ.

Prayer

Gracious God, who understands fully our strengths and limitations, thank you for not giving me any responsibility that is beyond your power to enable, strengthen, and encourage me. Amen.

SEEKING COUNSEL

From the Rule

Whenever any important business has to be done in the monastery, let the Abbot call together the whole community and state the matter to be acted upon. Then, having heard the brethren's advice, let him turn the matter over in his own mind and do what he shall judge to be most expedient. The reason we have said that all should be called for counsel is that the Lord often reveals to the younger what is best. Let the brethren give their advice with all the deference required by humility, and not presume stubbornly to defend their opinions; but let the decision rather depend on the Abbot's judgment, and all submit to whatever he shall decide for their welfare. However, just as it is proper for the disciples to obey their master, so also it is his function to dispose all things with prudence and justice. (Chapter 3, Part 1)

Proverbs 9

[9] Give instruction to the wise, and they will become wiser still;
   teach the righteous and they will gain in learning.
[10] The fear of the LORD is the beginning of wisdom,
   and the knowledge of the Holy One is insight.
[11] For by me your days will be multiplied,
   and years will be added to your life.

and from Proverbs 11

[2] When pride comes, then comes disgrace;
   but wisdom is with the humble.

Contemplation

1. What word, phrase, or image from these passages resonates with you?
2. What connection can you make to your own life?
3. What might God be calling you to do?

Reflection

The leadership style that Benedict is teaching isn't an autocratic one. What stands out in chapter 3 is the principle of humility, as modeled by the abbot in the way he or she leads. In important matters, Benedict advises, the abbot should seek the brothers' advice. Humility is also required of the older brothers in the acknowledgment that wisdom may come from the younger members of the community. Benedict urges his readers not to stubbornly defend their opinions (which brings to mind his injunction *to listen* in the Prologue).

Obedience is also relevant here. After seeking others' counsel, the abbot is the one who decides, and all should accept the decision and support the community and their leader in that decision. It is remarkable that twenty-first-century books on leadership would not be too much different in their advice to readers.

Prayer

Gracious God, give me the wisdom to seek council when I am making decisions that affect others and the humility to honor and support the decisions of those who lead me. May listening, love, and mutual obedience be present in our life together. Amen.

OTHERS IN AUTHORITY

From the Rule

To us, therefore, it seems expedient for the preservation of peace and charity that the Abbot have in his hands the full administration of his monastery. And if possible let all the affairs of the monastery, as we have already arranged, be administered by deans according to the Abbot's directions. Thus, with the duties being shared by several, no one person will become proud.

But if the circumstances of the place require it, or if the community asks for it with reason and with humility, and the Abbot judges it to be expedient, let the Abbot himself constitute as his Prior whomsoever he shall choose with the counsel of God-fearing brethren.

That Prior, however, shall perform respectfully the duties enjoined on him by his Abbot and do nothing against the Abbot's will or direction; for the more he is raised above the rest, the more carefully should he observe the precepts of the Rule.

If it should be found that the Prior has serious faults, or that he is deceived by his exaltation and yields to pride, or if he should be proved to be a despiser of the Holy Rule, let him be admonished verbally up to four times. If he fails to amend, let the correction of regular discipline be applied to him. But if even then he does not reform, let him be deposed from the office of Prior and another be appointed in his place who is worthy of it. And if afterwards he is not quiet and obedient in the community, let him even be expelled from the monastery. But the Abbot, for his part, should bear in mind that he will have to render an account to God for all his judgments, lest the flame of envy or jealousy be kindled in his soul. (Chapter 65, Part 2)

Acts 15

[35] But Paul and Barnabas remained in Antioch, and there, with many others, they taught and proclaimed the word of the Lord. [36] After some days Paul said to Barnabas, "Come, let us return and visit the believers in every city where we proclaimed the word of the Lord and see how they are doing." [37] Barnabas wanted to take with them John called Mark. [38] But Paul decided not to take with them one who had deserted them in Pamphylia and had not accompanied them in the work. [39] The disagreement became so sharp that they parted company; Barnabas took Mark with him and sailed away to Cyprus. [40] But Paul chose Silas and set out, the believers commending him to the grace of the Lord. [41] He went through Syria and Cilicia, strengthening the churches.

Contemplation

1. What word, phrase, or image from either of the two passages resonates with you?
2. What connection can you make to your own life?
3. What might God be calling you to do?

Reflection

Even the apostle Paul, it seems, had an issue with his second-in-command. Barnabas, who traveled and preached with Paul, was determined to take John Mark with them on their missions even though Paul was not convinced of the wisdom of that choice. As a result of their disagreement, they parted ways. Barnabas sailed to Cyprus with John Mark (who, according to tradition, was his cousin), and Paul took Silas as his companion as they journeyed through Syria and Cilicia. Barnabas is not mentioned again in the Acts of the Apostles.

It's not easy for a bright, ambitious second-in-command to defer to an authority figure who may at times be humanly fallible. Benedict must have included this advice in the Rule because of his own issues with some whom he appointed as priors. In chapter 3 of the Rule, Benedict made a point of stating that the abbot should take counsel from the whole community when making important decisions. But he also reminded the reader that the decision finally depends on the abbot's judgment. Humility again is required, both among those who follow and those who lead.

Prayer

Ruler of All, help me to appreciate those who are called by God to lead, and humbly submit to their authority as they shepherd our spiritual community. Amen.

CHALLENGING AUTHORITY

From the Rule

It happens all too often that the constituting of a Prior gives rise to grave scandals in monasteries. For there are some who become inflated with the evil spirit of pride and consider themselves second Abbots. By usurping power they foster scandals and cause dissensions in the community. Especially does this happen in those places where the Prior is constituted by the same Bishop or the same Abbots who constitute the Abbot himself. What an absurd procedure this is can easily be seen; for it gives the Prior an occasion for becoming proud from the very time of his constitution, by putting the thought into his mind that he is freed from the authority of his Abbot: "For," he will say to himself, "you were constituted by the same persons who constituted the Abbot." From this source are stirred up envy, quarrels, detraction, rivalry, dissensions, and disorders. For while the Abbot and the Prior are at variance, their souls cannot but be endangered by this dissension; and those who are under them, currying favor with one side or the other, go to ruin. The guilt for this dangerous state of affairs rests on the heads of those whose action brought about such disorder. (Chapter 65, Part 1)

Proverbs 16

16 How much better to get wisdom than gold!
   To get understanding is to be chosen rather than silver.
17 The highway of the upright avoids evil;
   those who guard their way preserve their lives.
18 Pride goes before destruction,
   and a haughty spirit before a fall.
19 It is better to be of a lowly spirit among the poor
   than to divide the spoil with the proud.
20 Those who are attentive to a matter will prosper,
   and happy are those who trust in the Lord.
21 The wise of heart is called perceptive,
   and pleasant speech increases persuasiveness.

Contemplation

1. What word, phrase, or image from either of the two passages resonates with you?
2. What connection can you make to your own life?
3. What might God be calling you to do?

Reflection

Who of us has not, at one time or another, had a boss at work of whom we thought, *What a foolish decision; I certainly could do better than that?* Benedict saw examples of this too. As abbot of at least twelve monasteries, he may have had priors who not only prided themselves as being better administrators than the abbot, but must have voiced this to others in the monastery as well. He must have had priors who attempted to usurp his authority and created dissension within the community, for this is what he writes about in this chapter.

However, Benedict writes, our "own souls are inevitably endangered by this discord." As my mother said to me many times as I grew up (not getting the quote from Proverbs exactly right), "Pride goeth before a fall." This was usually said after I contradicted her or was critical of others in my family.

The warning about pride is consistent with Benedict's theme of humility that runs through the entire Rule, from the prologue, through chapter 7 on humility (the longest chapter in the Rule), and now pops up in this chapter. Humility is certainly implied in the chapters on the assignment of impossible tasks (chapter 68) and mutual obedience (chapter 71). Benedict's teaching on the role of the abbot and the role of the prior establishes a model of servant leadership.

Prayer

Help me, Loving God, to always maintain a reverence for your teaching and to maintain an appropriate humility in my response to my leaders and my interactions with my brothers and sisters in Christ. Amen.

ASSISTING IN LEADERSHIP

From the Rule

If the community is a large one, let there be chosen out of it brethren of good repute and holy life, and let them be appointed deans. These shall take charge of their deaneries in all things, observing the commandments of God and the instructions of their Abbot.

Let men of such character be chosen deans that the Abbot may with confidence share his burdens among them. Let them be chosen not by rank but according to their worthiness of life and the wisdom of their doctrine.

If any of these deans should become inflated with pride and found deserving of censure, let him be corrected once, and again, and a third time. If he will not amend, then let him be deposed and another be put in his place who is worthy of it.

And we order the same to be done in the case of the Prior. (Chapter 21)

Matthew 10

[5] These twelve Jesus sent out with the following instructions: "Go nowhere among the Gentiles, and enter no town of the Samaritans, [6] but go rather to the lost sheep of the house of Israel. [7] As you go, proclaim the good news, 'The kingdom of heaven has come near.' [8] Cure the sick, raise the dead, cleanse the lepers, cast out

demons. You received without payment; give without payment. [9] Take no gold, or silver, or copper in your belts, [10] no bag for your journey, or two tunics, or sandals, or a staff; for laborers deserve their food. [11] Whatever town or village you enter, find out who in it is worthy, and stay there until you leave. [12] As you enter the house, greet it. [13] If the house is worthy, let your peace come upon it; but if it is not worthy, let your peace return to you.

Contemplation

1. What word, phrase, or image from either of the two passages resonates with you?
2. What connection can you make to your own life?
3. What might God be calling you to do?

Reflection

In chapter 2 of the Rule, Benedict wrote "The abbot is believed to hold the place of Christ in the monastery" (RSB 2:2). So, it is fitting that leadership in a monastic community should follow the pattern that Christ himself set. As his ministry grew, Jesus chose twelve to assist him. Similarly, in the spirit of practicality and balance so characteristic of the Rule, Benedict makes provision for the abbot to appoint "deans" to oversee and give more personal attention to small groups of members. These leaders should be the kind of persons with whom the abbot can confidently share the burdens of leadership.

The Gospels, whether in Matthew, Mark or Luke, do not really say what the qualifications for apostleship are, and it seems that Christ chose a rather motley crew who, with the exception perhaps of Matthew, the tax collector, had little leadership promise. Apparently, little was needed. Christ told them to take no money, no food, no bag of clothes. What they needed would be provided.

Benedict simply says that deans should be "chosen for virtuous living and wise teaching, not for their rank." In addition, the only real qualification for spiritual leadership is obedience and a willingness to follow. Many leaders step into their roles unsure of their worthiness to lead, only to discover that God's grace is all they need.

Prayer

Gracious God, look with favor on those who are called to lead. Give them a heart for others and willingness to follow Christ. Amen.

THE MAKING OF A PRIEST

From the Rule

If an Abbot desire to have a priest or a deacon ordained for his monastery, let him choose one of his monks who is worthy to exercise the priestly office.

But let the one who is ordained beware of self-exaltation or pride; and let him not presume to do anything except what is commanded him by the Abbot, knowing that he is so much the more subject to the discipline of the Rule. Nor should he by reason of his priesthood forget the obedience and the discipline required by the Rule, but make ever more and more progress toward God.

Let him always keep the place which he received on entering the monastery, except in his duties at the altar or in case the choice of the community and the will of the Abbot should promote him for the worthiness of his life. Yet he must understand that he is to observe the rules laid down by deans and Priors.

Should he presume to act otherwise, let him be judged not as a priest but as a rebel. And if he does not reform after repeated admonitions, let even the Bishop be brought in as a witness. If then he still fails to amend, and his offenses are notorious, let him be put out of the monastery, but only if his contumacy is such that he refuses to submit or to obey the Rule. (Chapter 62)

Exodus 40

[12] Then you shall bring Aaron and his sons to the entrance of the tent of meeting, and shall wash them with water, [13] and put on Aaron the sacred vestments, and you shall anoint him and consecrate him, so that he may serve me as priest. [14] You shall bring his sons also and put tunics on them, [15] and anoint them, as you anointed their father, that they may serve me as priests: and their anointing shall admit them to a perpetual priesthood throughout all generations to come.

Contemplation

1. What word, phrase, or image from either of the two passages resonates with you?
2. What connection can you make to your own life?
3. What might God be calling you to do?

Reflection

Exodus 40 shows us that the tradition of choosing someone to be a priest from among the community goes back a long way. As skeptical as Benedict seemed to be of priests in the monastery, there were and continue to be practical reasons for having a priest. For example, it is common in most monasteries to celebrate Eucharist every day, and a priest is needed to say the absolution, consecrate the elements, and give the blessing. Benedict cautions, however, that the monk ordained as a priest "must be on guard against conceit or pride" and still falls under the authority of the abbot.

Not all priestly duties are unique responsibilities. All baptized persons share in the priestly ministry of Christ. When writing to exiled Christians throughout the Roman empire, Peter referred to them as a "royal priesthood" (1 Peter 2:9). This means that all followers of Christ have a duty to proclaim the Gospel, pray for and minister to others, and build the kingdom of God. The Book of Common Prayer also levels the status of priests as one of several kinds of ministry, including lay ministry. The most effective priests I have known have been those who serve with humility, not claiming privilege and honoring others' ministry for its importance to the body of Christ.

Prayer

Holy God, grant me the grace and wisdom to find my ministry as part of Christ's "royal priesthood" and to serve with diligence and humility. Amen.

WATCHING AT THE GATES

From the Rule

At the gate of the monastery let there be placed a wise old man, who knows how to receive and to give a message, and whose maturity will prevent him from straying about. This porter should have a room near the gate, so that those who come may always find someone at hand to attend to their business. And as soon as anyone knocks or a poor man hails him, let him answer "Thanks be to God" or "A blessing!" Then let him attend to them promptly, with all the meekness inspired by the fear of God and with the warmth of charity.

Should the porter need help, let him have one of the younger brethren.

If it can be done, the monastery should be so established that all the necessary things, such as water, mill, garden, and various workshops, may be within the enclosure, so that there is no necessity for the monks to go about outside of it, since that is not at all profitable for their souls.

We desire that this Rule be read often in the community, so that none of the brethren may excuse himself on the ground of ignorance. (Chapter 66)

Proverbs 8

[32] And now, my children, listen to me:
   happy are those who keep my ways.
[33] Hear instruction and be wise,
   and do not neglect it.
[34] Happy is the one who listens to me,
   watching daily at my gates,
   waiting beside my doors.
[35] For whoever finds me finds life
   and obtains favor from the LORD;
[36] but those who miss me injure themselves;
   all who hate me love death.

Contemplation

1. What word, phrase, or image from either of the two passages resonates with you?
2. What connection can you make to your own life?
3. What might God be calling you to do?

Reflection

The reader of this chapter has to keep in mind chapter 53 of the Rule on the reception of guests. Remember that Benedictine hospitality requires that all who arrive "be received like Christ." A prayer and a kiss of peace should be offered. Benedict instructs the porter to give salutations to "all guests, whether arriving or departing" with complete humility and a bowed head.

The porter had the important functions of receiving guests and keeping restless monks within the monastery, so it must have been a careful process to select a sensible older monk who could be no-nonsense about guarding the entrance and delivering messages to the abbot and prior but, at the same time, retain the gentleness and "warmth of love" required by the job of greeting visitors.

The other interesting thing about this chapter is the instruction on how monasteries should be built to be self-sustaining compounds, having their own water source, mill, and garden. Benedict set the standard for all monasteries that were established after his own. In the early ninth century, Louis the Pious, son of the emperor Charlemagne, declared that the Rule of Benedict would be the blueprint of organization for all monastic communities.

Prayer

Gracious God, who loves each of us as his own child, help me to be gentle, humble, and loving in my interactions with others, even as I am busy with important tasks. Amen.

BEING RESPONSIBLE

From the Rule

As cellarer of the monastery let there be chosen from the community one who is wise, of mature character, sober, not a great eater, not haughty, not excitable, not offensive, not slow, not wasteful, but a God-fearing man who may be like a father to the whole community. Let him have charge of everything. He shall do nothing without the Abbot's orders, but keep to his instructions. Let him not vex the brethren. If any brother happens to make some unreasonable demand of him, instead of vexing the brother with a contemptuous refusal he should humbly give the reason for denying the improper request. Let him keep guard over his own soul, mindful always of the Apostle's saying that "he who has ministered well will acquire for himself a good standing" (1 Tim. 3:13). Let him take the greatest care of the sick, of children, of guests and of the poor, knowing without doubt that he will have to render an account for all these on the Day of Judgment. Let him regard all the utensils of the monastery and its whole property as if they were the sacred vessels of the altar. Let him not think that he may neglect anything. He should be neither a miser nor a prodigal and squanderer of the monastery's substance, but should do all things with measure and in accordance with the Abbot's instructions. (Chapter 31)

Genesis 39

[2] The LORD was with Joseph, and he became a successful man; he was in the house of his Egyptian master. [3] His master saw that the LORD was with him, and that the LORD caused all that he did to prosper in his hands. [4] So Joseph found favor in his sight and attended him; he made him overseer of his house and put him in charge of all that he had. [5] From the time that he made him overseer in his house and over all that he had, the LORD blessed the Egyptian's house for Joseph's sake; the blessing of the LORD was on all that he had, in house and field. [6] So he left all that he had in Joseph's charge; and, with him there, he had no concern for anything but the food that he ate.

Contemplation

1. What word, phrase, or image from either of the two passages resonates with you?
2. What connection can you make to your own life?
3. What might God be calling you to do?

Reflection

What kind of person would you want to be in charge of all the monastery's food and supplies? According to Benedict, one who is wise, mature, even-tempered, respectful, obedient ("do nothing without the Abbot's orders"), compassionate (taking "greatest care of the sick, of children, of guests and of the poor"), of devout faith—in other words, a perfect servant.

What kind of person do I want to be? A faithful cellarer—one who oversees the tools, utensils, and supplies "in house and field"—wouldn't be a bad standard to aspire to. As the passage from Genesis 39 suggests, an overseer is an important role. Am I ready to take on a role requiring responsibility in my spiritual community? How well do I manage my role as a family member or spouse? Am I self-controlled, being thoughtful and loving in my interactions with others? The most important criterion may well be keeping guard over one's own soul. If I am faithful in my prayer and devotion, the fruits of the Spirit may well follow: love, joy, peace, forbearance, kindness, goodness, faithfulness, gentleness, and self-control (Gal. 5:22–23).

Prayer

Great teacher and guide, draw me continually to you, and mold me into the faithful servant you would have me to be. Amen.

8

⸏

DISCIPLINE

DISCIPLINING DISCIPLES

From the Rule

In his teaching the Abbot should always follow the Apostle's formula: "Reprove, entreat, rebuke" (2 Tim. 4:2); threatening at one time and coaxing at another as the occasion may require, showing now the stern countenance of a master, now the loving affection of a father. That is to say, it is the undisciplined and restless whom he must reprove rather sharply; it is the obedient, meek, and patient whom he must entreat to advance in virtue; while as for the negligent and disdainful, these we charge him to rebuke and correct.

And let him not shut his eyes to the faults of offenders; but, since he has the authority, let him cut out those faults by the roots as soon as they begin to appear, remembering the fate of Heli, the priest of Silo (1 Kings 2–4). The well-disposed and those of good understanding let him correct with verbal admonition the first and second time. But bold, hard, proud, and disobedient characters he should curb at the very beginning of their ill-doing by stripes and other bodily punishments, knowing that it is written, "the fool is not corrected with words" (Prov. 18:2; 29:19), and again, "Beat your son with the rod, and you will deliver his soul from death" (Prov. 23:13–14). (Chapter 2, Part 5)

2 Timothy 4

In the presence of God and of Christ Jesus, who is to judge the living and the dead, and in view of his appearing and his kingdom, I solemnly urge you: ² proclaim the message; be persistent whether the time is favorable or unfavorable; convince, rebuke, and encourage, with the utmost patience in teaching. ³ For the time is coming when people will not put up with sound doctrine, but having itching ears, they will accumulate for themselves teachers to suit their own desires, ⁴ and will turn away from listening to the truth and wander away to myths. ⁵ As for you, always be sober, endure suffering, do the work of an evangelist, carry out your ministry fully.

Contemplation

1. What word, phrase, or image from either of the two passages resonates with you?
2. What connection can you make to your own life?
3. What might God be calling you to do?

Reflection

It is easy to be distracted by the startling admonition to beat the disobedient monks or use other "bodily punishments." We must remember that Benedict wrote this in the sixth century, a brutal time, long before the study of psychology and before corporal punishment would no longer be acceptable practice.

But the overriding message here is to deal with each person individually, knowing that some require only coaxing or a soft admonition. Those who are more disdainful or stubborn will need stronger measures. This is one of many passages in the Rule that exemplifies the balance characteristic in Benedict's teaching. Exceptions can always be made, flexibility is always required, and everything should be thoughtfully done in the spirit of love. What is not allowable is to overlook negligence or disobedience. The health of the community depends on addressing those issues.

Prayer

Ruler of the Universe, we pray for the health of our faith community and for its leaders, that they may be attentive to our needs, encourage us when we fall behind, and lovingly discipline us when we stray. Amen.

THE WORK OF GOD

From the Rule

At the hour for the Divine Office, as soon as the signal is heard, let them abandon whatever they may have in hand and hasten with the greatest speed, yet with seriousness, so that there is no excuse for levity. Let nothing, therefore, be put before the Work of God.

If at the Night Office anyone arrives after the "Glory be to the Father" of Psalm 94—which Psalm for this reason we wish to be said very slowly and protractedly— let him not stand in his usual place in the choir; but let him stand last of all, or in a place set aside by the Abbot for such negligent ones in order that they may be seen by him and by all. He shall remain there until the Work of God has been completed, and then do penance by a public satisfaction. The reason why we have judged it fitting for them so stand in the last place or in a place apart is that, being seen by all, they may amend for very shame. For if they remain outside of the oratory, there will perhaps be someone who will go back to bed and sleep or at least seat himself outside and indulge in idle talk, and thus an occasion will be provided for the evil one. But let them go inside, that they many not lose the whole Office, and may amend for the future.

At the day Hours anyone who does not arrive at the Work of God until after the verse and the "Glory be to the Father" for the first Psalm following it shall stand in the last place, according to our ruling above. Nor shall he presume to join the choir in their chanting until he has made satisfaction, unless the Abbot should pardon him and give him permission; but even then the offender must make satisfaction for his fault. (Chapter 43, Part 1)

Psalm 95

¹ O come, let us sing to the LORD;
  let us make a joyful noise to the rock of our salvation!
² Let us come into his presence with thanksgiving;
  let us make a joyful noise to him with songs of praise!
³ For the LORD is a great God,
  and a great King above all gods.
⁴ In his hand are the depths of the earth;
  the heights of the mountains are his also.
⁵ The sea is his, for he made it,
  and the dry land, which his hands have formed.
⁶ O come, let us worship and bow down,
  let us kneel before the LORD, our Maker!
⁷ For he is our God,
  and we are the people of his pasture,
  and the sheep of his hand.
  O that today you would listen to his voice!

Contemplation

1. What word, phrase, or image from either of the two passages resonates with you?
2. What connection can you make to your own life?
3. What might God be calling you to do?

Reflection

Benedict makes it clear that the most important role of the monastery is the work of God (*opus dei*). Nothing should come before it, and it should be taken very seriously ("hasten . . . with seriousness . . . there is no excuse for levity"). In monastic speak, the *opus dei* is the Divine Office, or the seven services of prayer, some long and some short, that are scheduled throughout the day, from before dawn until nightfall. The practice dates back to the early church. The early Christians (who were Jews) prayed the Psalms and other scripture texts, especially in the morning and evening, as they continue to do. The practice of frequent prayer was fully in keeping with Paul's injunction to "pray without ceasing," found in his First Letter to the Thessalonians.

Today, Morning Prayer still begins with the *Venite*, or Psalm 95. (In Benedict's Bible it was numbered as 94.) In the graciousness that was typical of Benedict, he demanded punctuality, but allowed for monks to slip in before the Venite was finished before punishment for tardiness would be administered. Today monks still stop whatever they are doing when they hear the bell for the Divine Office, and hurry to the chapel, because nothing is more important than prayer. The practice is not just for monks. As Joan Chittister reminds us, "There is nothing more important in our own list of important things to do in life than to stop at regular intervals, in regular ways to remember what life is really about . . . and for whom we are to live it."[1]

Prayer

Gracious God, remind me during my busy day to stop, to remember what is important and to whom I belong. Amen.

TAKING A TIME-OUT

From the Rule

If a brother is found to be obstinate, or disobedient, or proud, or murmuring, or habitually transgressing the Holy Rule in any point and contemptuous of the orders of his seniors, the latter shall admonish him secretly a first and a second time, as Our Lord commands (Matt 18:15–16). If he fails to amend, let him be given a public rebuke in front of the whole community. But if even then he does not reform, let him be placed under excommunication, provided that he

---

1. Chittister, *Rule of Benedict*, 126.

understands the seriousness of that penalty; if he is perverse, however, let him undergo corporal punishment. (Chapter 23)

Matthew 18

[15] "If another member of the church sins against you, go and point out the fault when the two of you are alone. If the member listens to you, you have regained that one. [16] But if you are not listened to, take one or two others along with you, so that every word may be confirmed by the evidence of two or three witnesses. [17] If the member refuses to listen to them, tell it to the church; and if the offender refuses to listen even to the church, let such a one be to you as a Gentile and a tax collector. [18] Truly I tell you, whatever you bind on earth will be bound in heaven, and whatever you loose on earth will be loosed in heaven."

Contemplation

1. What word, phrase, or image from either of the two passages resonates with you?
2. What connection can you make to your own life?
3. What might God be calling you to do?

Reflection

Dealing with disrupters or rule-breakers within a group or organization must be one of the hardest things a leader has to do. This chapter reminds us that not everyone who enters a monastery is a saint. People had several reasons for entering monasteries. Medieval monasteries were places of sanctuary in sometimes tumultuous areas where city-states would take up arms against neighboring city-states. Monasteries offered education mainly to boys, some of whom were looking to become priests or monastics and others who were looking to enter other professions.

And so, the need for discipline was a given in those communities. Benedict, as he did for other issues, wisely followed scriptural teaching on the matter: warn the person privately before making the matter public. Some will listen and accept correction. The real challenge is with those who don't. The term "excommunication," as Benedict uses it here, refers to temporary isolation, as becomes clear in subsequent chapters of the Rule.

Looking at this teaching from the standpoint of one who often bristles when corrected, I realize that my part in preserving the integrity of the community is as important as the leader's. Can I, with humility, hear the concern, make amends, and change my ways? If not, the leader should be wise enough to know when to isolate the offender to spare the community.

Prayer

Strengthen and guide our spiritual leaders. Give them wisdom in dealing with conflict and disobedience. Help me to always understand my place in the community and with humility listen to criticism, accept discipline, and change my ways for the good of others. Amen.

OUR RESPONSE TO DISCIPLINE

From the Rule

The measure of excommunication or of chastisement should correspond to the degree of fault, which degree is estimated by the Abbot's judgment. If a brother is found guilty of lighter faults, let him be excluded from the common table. Now the program for one deprived of the fellowship of the table shall be as follows: In the oratory he shall intone neither Psalm nor antiphon nor shall he recite a lesson until he has made satisfaction; in the refectory he shall take his food alone after the community meal, so that if the brethren eat at the sixth hour, for instance, that brother shall eat at the ninth, while if they eat at the ninth hour he shall eat in the evening, until by a suitable satisfaction he obtains pardon. (Chapter 24)

Hebrews 12

[6] "For the Lord disciplines those whom he loves, and chastises every child whom he accepts." [7] Endure trials for the sake of discipline. God is treating you as children; for what child is there whom a parent does not discipline? [8] If you do not have that discipline in which all children share, then you are illegitimate and not his children. [9] Moreover, we had human parents to discipline us, and we respected them. Should we not be even more willing to be subject to the Father of spirits and live? [10] For they disciplined us for a short time as seemed best to them, but he disciplines us for our good, in order that we may share his holiness. [11] Now, discipline always seems painful rather than pleasant at the time, but later it yields the peaceful fruit of righteousness to those who have been trained by it.

Contemplation

1. What word, phrase, or image from either of the two passages resonates with you?
2. What connection can you make to your own life?
3. What might God be calling you to do?

Reflection

The first step in the continuum of punishments, after warnings, is a time-out: not being able to eat with the others or participate in the liturgy. As former abbot Philip Lawrence of Christ in the Desert writes, a literal reading of this rule may not work today, living as we do in highly individualistic times, when a monk can be quite happy to be "excused" from the common table,[2] eating alone instead. But the principle still applies: discipline should be proportionate to the offense. The abbot (or abbess) should be judicious in the use of discipline, in keeping with Benedict's theme of balance throughout The Rule. Discipline is administered hand-in-hand with mercy, and everything should be done in love.

The principle in the passage from Hebrews also is balanced in the way we respond to the Lord's discipline. We are not, on the one hand, to regard it lightly or, on the other hand, to "faint" when God reproves us. We should neither be dismissive nor disheartened when our faults are pointed out to us and we suffer the consequences of our actions. After all, says the writer of Hebrews, "For the Lord disciplines those whom he loves." God's discipline is evidence of God's love. As Hebrews 12 tells us, "He disciplines us for our good, in order that we may share His holiness."

Prayer

Wise and loving God, help me to embrace your discipline, never disregarding it or letting it overwhelm and discourage me. Help me to realize that your correction is a sign of your love, bringing me to share in your holiness. Amen.

THE BODY'S RESPONSE

From the Rule

One who for serious faults is excommunicated from oratory and table shall make satisfaction as follows. At the hour when the celebration of the Work of God is concluded in the oratory, let him lie prostrate before the door of the oratory, saying nothing, but only lying prone with his face to the ground at the feet of all as they come out of the oratory. And let him continue to do this until the Abbot judges that satisfaction has been made. Then, when he has come at the Abbot's bidding, let him cast himself first at the Abbot's feet and then at the feet of all, that they may pray for him.

---

2. Philip Lawrence, OSB, "Commentary on Chapter 24: Degrees of Excommunication," from the website of the Monastery of Christ in the Desert. Accessed March 5, 2017, https://christdesert.org/prayer/rule-of-st-benedict/chapter-24-degrees-of-excommunication/.

And next, if the Abbot so orders, let him be received into the choir, to the place which the Abbot appoints, but with the provision that he shall not presume to intone Psalm or lesson or anything else in the oratory without a further order from the Abbot. Moreover, at every Hour, when the Work of God is ended, let him cast himself on the ground in the place where he stands. And let him continue to satisfy in this way until the Abbot again orders him finally to cease from this satisfaction.

But those who for slight faults are excommunicated only from table shall make satisfaction in the oratory, and continue in it till an order from the Abbot, until he blesses them and says, "It is enough." (Chapter 44)

1 Kings 18

[36] At the time of the offering of the oblation, the prophet Elijah came near and said, "O Lord, God of Abraham, Isaac, and Israel, let it be known this day that you are God in Israel, that I am your servant, and that I have done all these things at your bidding. [37] Answer me, O Lord, answer me, so that this people may know that you, O Lord, are God, and that you have turned their hearts back." [38] Then the fire of the Lord fell and consumed the burnt offering, the wood, the stones, and the dust, and even licked up the water that was in the trench. [39] When all the people saw it, they fell on their faces and said, "The Lord indeed is God; the Lord indeed is God."

Contemplation

1. What word, phrase, or image from either of the two passages resonates with you?
2. What connection can you make to your own life?
3. What might God be calling you to do?

Reflection

Worshippers in many major world religions employ prostration as an act of submissiveness or worship to a supreme being. The position of the body and its parts was considered very important as ways to elicit a proper emotional response during times of devotion. The *De Penitentia* of Peter the Chanter[3] (d. 1197) listed at least seven different prayer postures; some involved standing with hands arranged in various positions of strain, one involved kneeling, and two others involved lying prostrate on the ground.

---

3. "Piety," *The Oxford Encyclopedia of the Reformation* (Oxford, UK: Oxford University Press, 2005).

It is interesting that Benedict recommends this posture as the response of a penitent monk who has been isolated as punishment and wants to get back into the good graces and life of the community. Prostration is the posture of penitence and is still practiced today in many cultures. The twenty-first-century version I have observed in a Western monastery does not require full prostration, but simply kneeling before the altar.

However, the act of prostration as it is found in scripture is more often the response of someone who is awed by a sudden realization of God's power and majesty, as in the scripture passage above. Isn't it wonderful to think of repentance as not merely acknowledging one's wrongfulness and a desire to return to fellowship, but as a new realization of who God is?

Prayer

Gracious Father who is always ready to forgive, may sin never make me blind to who you are, and when I stray, always lead me back into your glorious presence. Amen.

DRAWING THE LINE

From the Rule

Let the brother who is guilty of a weightier fault be excluded both from the table and from the oratory. Let none of the brethren join him either for company or for conversation. Let him be alone at the work assigned him, abiding in penitential sorrow and pondering that terrible sentence of the Apostle where he says that a man of that kind is handed over for the destruction of the flesh, that the spirit may be saved in the day of the Lord (1 Cor. 5:5). Let him take his meals alone in the measure and at the hour which the Abbot shall consider suitable for him. He shall not be blessed by those who pass by, nor shall the food that is given him be blessed. (Chapter 25)

1 Corinthians 5

3 For though absent in body, I am present in spirit; and as if present I have already pronounced judgment 4 in the name of the Lord Jesus on the man who has done such a thing.[a] When you are assembled, and my spirit is present with the power of our Lord Jesus, 5 you are to hand this man over to Satan for the destruction of the flesh, so that his spirit may be saved in the day of the Lord.[b]

⁶ Your boasting is not a good thing. Do you not know that a little yeast leavens the whole batch of dough? ⁷ Clean out the old yeast so that you may be a new batch, as you really are unleavened. For our paschal lamb, Christ, has been sacrificed. ⁸ Therefore, let us celebrate the festival, not with the old yeast, the yeast of malice and evil, but with the unleavened bread of sincerity and truth.

⁹ I wrote to you in my letter not to associate with sexually immoral persons— ¹⁰ not at all meaning the immoral of this world, or the greedy and robbers, or idolaters, since you would then need to go out of the world. ¹¹ But now I am writing to you not to associate with anyone who bears the name of brother or sister[c] who is sexually immoral or greedy, or is an idolater, reviler, drunkard, or robber. Do not even eat with such a one. ¹² For what have I to do with judging those outside? Is it not those who are inside that you are to judge? ¹³ God will judge those outside. "Drive out the wicked person from among you."

Contemplation

1. What word, phrase, or image from either of the two passages resonates with you?
2. What connection can you make to your own life?
3. What might God be calling you to do?

Reflection

When do we draw the line, say enough is enough, realize that our response, motivated by mercy and forgiveness, is not leading to better behavior and is, in fact, having a destructive effect on the community? This is the question Benedict must have had to ask himself as an abbot dealing with recalcitrant monks. The apostle Paul seems to have reached this point when talking about the member of the Corinthian church who seems to have gone beyond recalcitrance into unrepentant immorality. In our time, these issues often turn into questions about codependence. To what degree are we supporting the bad behavior by softening the consequences?

When immersed in conversations about love, mercy, and forgiveness, we must remind ourselves that love sometimes requires doing the hard thing. *Balance* requires it. The point may come when we can no longer tolerate an intolerable situation and must abandon the unrepentant one for the sake of the community.

Prayer

Merciful God, bless and guard our community of faith. Help us always to uphold standards of right behavior. Help me to know when I have to turn away someone I care about, but remind me also to pray for those who have lost their way. Amen.

UPHOLDING A DECISION

From the Rule

If any brother presumes without an order from the Abbot to associate in any way with an excommunicated brother, or to speak with him, or to send him a message, he should receive a similar punishment of excommunication. (Chapter 26)

Titus 3

[1] Remind them to be subject to rulers and authorities, to be obedient, to be ready for every good work, [2] to speak evil of no one, to avoid quarreling, to be gentle, and to show every courtesy to everyone. [3] For we ourselves were once foolish, disobedient, led astray, slaves to various passions and pleasures, passing our days in malice and envy, despicable, hating one another. [4] But when the goodness and loving kindness of God our Savior appeared, [5] he saved us, not because of any works of righteousness that we had done, but according to his mercy, through the water of rebirth and renewal by the Holy Spirit. [6] This Spirit he poured out on us richly through Jesus Christ our Savior, [7] so that, having been justified by his grace, we might become heirs according to the hope of eternal life. [8] The saying is sure. I desire that you insist on these things, so that those who have come to believe in God may be careful to devote themselves to good works; these things are excellent and profitable to everyone. [9] But avoid stupid controversies, genealogies, dissensions, and quarrels about the law, for they are unprofitable and worthless. [10] After a first and second admonition, have nothing more to do with anyone who causes divisions, [11] since you know that such a person is perverted and sinful, being self-condemned.

Contemplation

1. What word, phrase, or image from either of the two passages resonates with you?
2. What connection can you make to your own life?
3. What might God be calling you to do?

Reflection

The chapters on excommunication are among Benedict's hardest teachings, and I find it difficult to embrace them. However, the impulse to forgive and welcome back must be weighed against the detrimental effect to the community of one who causes dissension. We must remember that this person was excommunicated not for a first offense, or for two, but for a pattern of creating disruption.

Benedict is making a statement about undermining the authority of the abbot. The monastery is not a democratic community; it is a sacramental community in which the abbot "holds the place of Christ."

Prayer

Holy God, help me to support and uphold your kingdom. I bring before you the members of my community, remembering especially those who have wandered from your way. May I be obedient in fulfilling my responsibility toward them. Amen.

LOVE AND HOPE

From the Rule

Let the Abbot be most solicitous in his concern for delinquent brethren, for "it is not the healthy but the sick who need a physician" (Matt 9:12). And therefore he ought to use every means that a wise physician would use. Let him send "senpectae," that is, brethren of mature years and wisdom, who may as it were secretly console the wavering brother and induce him to make humble satisfaction; comforting him that he may not "be overwhelmed by excessive grief" (2 Cor. 2:7) but that, as the Apostle says, charity may be strengthened in him (2 Cor. 2:8). And let everyone pray for him.

For the Abbot must have the utmost solicitude and exercise all prudence and diligence lest he lose any of the sheep entrusted to him. Let him know that what he has undertaken is the care of weak souls and not a tyranny over strong ones; and let him fear the Prophet's warning through which God says, "What you saw to be fat you took to yourselves, and what was feeble you cast away" (Ezek. 34:3–4). Let him rather imitate the loving example of the Good Shepherd who left the ninety-nine sheep in the mountains and went to look for the one sheep that had gone astray, on whose weakness He had such compassion that He deigned to place it on His own sacred shoulders and thus carry it back to the flock (Luke 15:5). (Chapter 27)

Luke 15

Now all the tax collectors and sinners were coming near to listen to him. [2] And the Pharisees and the scribes were grumbling and saying, "This fellow welcomes sinners and eats with them." [3] So he told them this parable: [4] "Which one of you, having a hundred sheep and losing one of them, does not leave the ninety-nine in the wilderness and go after the one that is lost until he finds it? [5] When he has found it, he lays it on his shoulders and rejoices. [6] And when he comes home, he calls together his friends and neighbors, saying to them, 'Rejoice with me, for I have found my sheep that was lost.' [7] Just so, I tell you, there will be more joy in heaven over one sinner who repents than over ninety-nine righteous persons who need no repentance."

Contemplation

1. What word, phrase, or image from either of the two passages resonates with you?
2. What connection can you make to your own life?
3. What might God be calling you to do?

Reflection

Sending someone away for the sake of the community does not mean that the one who is banished is gone from our hearts and our prayers. Love and, when needed, care follow that one as long as they are needed.

Easier said than done, right? Often, the excommunication is accompanied by feelings of disappointment—if not anger and disgust—toward the offender. We don't necessarily want to think about that person again or be reminded of the offenses that led to the decision for exclusion. Our response is good riddance.

But this is not Jesus's teaching or the guidance from Benedict. Jesus taught us to love our enemies. His examples of the prodigal son and parable of the good shepherd tell us to leave open the hope for repentance and return of the one who has grieved us.

Prayer

Merciful God, help me to love the sinner and welcome back the lost one. Amen.

TEAR IT OUT

From the Rule

If a brother who has been frequently corrected for some fault, and even excommunicated, does not amend, let a harsher correction be applied, that is, let the punishment of the rod be administered. But if he still does not reform or perhaps (which God forbid) even becomes proud and actually defends his conduct, then let the Abbot do what a wise physician would do. Having used applications, the ointments of exhortation, the medicines of the Holy Scriptures, finally the cautery of excommunication and of the strokes of the rod, if he sees that his efforts are of no avail, let him apply a still greater remedy, his own prayers and those of all the others, that the Lord, who can do all things may restore health to the brother who is sick. But if he is not healed even in this way, then let the Abbot use the knife of amputation, according to the Apostle's words, "Expel the evil one from your midst" (1 Cor. 5:13), and again, "If the faithless one departs, let him depart" (1 Cor. 7:15) lest one diseased sheep infect the whole flock. (Chapter 28)

1 Corinthians 5

[11] But now I am writing to you not to associate with anyone who bears the name of brother or sister who is sexually immoral or greedy, or is an idolater, reviler, drunkard, or robber. Do not even eat with such a one. [12] For what have I to do with judging those outside? Is it not those who are inside that you are to judge? [13] God will judge those outside. "Drive out the wicked person from among you."

Contemplation

1. What word, phrase, or image from either of the two passages resonates with you?
2. What connection can you make to your own life?
3. What might God be calling you to do?

Reflection

Of all the chapters in the Rule, this one is probably my least favorite. The practices of excommunication and beating with a rod are not ones we readily embrace today and seem to be contrary to the Gospel of inclusion and forgiveness. And it is hard to think of anyone beyond the reach of prayer.

Up to this point, Benedict has referred to the wayward brother or sister as one who is sick (RSB 27). Here he draws a line between the spiritually sick and the hardened unrepentant whose behaviors and attitude even the rod does not change. Today, monasteries do not administer the rod, but occasionally monks are counseled to leave if it is clear that they are not inclined to conform to community standards or monastic life.

Accommodating individual differences and forgiveness of others' faults can only go so far. Above all, the emotional health and spiritual well-being of the community take priority. Remember that Jesus told his disciples "if your eye causes you to stumble, tear it out; it is better for you to enter the kingdom of God with one eye than to have two eyes and to be thrown into hell" (Mark 9:47).

Prayer

Righteous God, watch over our community and guide the ones who are lost. Help me to see things as you see them as I remember the troubled ones in prayer. Amen.

WHEN TO SPEAK OUT

From the Rule

Care must be taken that no monk presume on any ground to defend another monk in the monastery, or as it were to take him under his protection, even though they be united by some tie of blood-relationship. Let not the monks dare to do this in any way whatsoever, because it may give rise to most serious scandals. But if anyone breaks this rule, let him be severely punished. (Chapter 69)

Proverbs 31

8 Speak out for those who cannot speak,
  for the rights of all the destitute.
9 Speak out, judge righteously,
  defend the rights of the poor and needy.

and Acts 7

23 When [Moses] was forty years old, it came into his heart to visit his relatives, the Israelites. 24 When he saw one of them being wronged, he defended the oppressed man and avenged him by striking down the Egyptian. 25 He supposed that his kinsfolk would understand that God through him was rescuing them, but they did not understand. 26 The next day he came to some of them as they were quarreling and tried to reconcile them, saying, "Men, you are brothers; why do you wrong each other?" 27 But the man who was wronging his neighbor pushed Moses aside, saying, "Who made you a ruler and a judge over us? 28 Do you want to kill me as you killed the Egyptian yesterday?" 29 When he heard this, Moses fled and became a resident alien in the land of Midian.

Contemplation

1. What word, phrase, or image from these three passages resonates with you?
2. What connection can you make to your own life?
3. What might God be calling you to do?

Reflection

The Bible seems to say two different things when it comes to defending another. The passage from Proverbs says we are to speak out on behalf of the poor, needy, and those who cannot speak on their own behalf. But the Acts account, where Stephen is telling the story of Moses, relays a cautionary tale about defending another person. In defending another, Moses committed a sin himself, in fact, killing the oppressor.

Two reasons exist why we should proceed cautiously when coming to another's defense. The first is that, in the heat of the moment, you may say or do something that exacerbates the situation and, like Moses, commit a grievous offense yourself. Acting from our outrage always carries with it unintended consequences. In John's gospel (chapter 18), Peter coming to the defense of Jesus in the garden led him to cut off the ear of the high priest's slave, and Jesus rebuked him.

The second reason one should be cautious in defending another is that you may be acting out of only partial knowledge and interfering with something else that needs to happen. I have sometimes become heated in defending another person, only to find out later that there was another side to the story. The persons we defend aren't always blameless. And I think this is Benedict's point. Monks take a vow of obedience: obedience to God, obedience to the abbot, and obedience to each other. In taking sides with someone you've taken under your wing, you may in fact not be considering the needs of others or honoring the authority of the abbot (or leader).

Prayer

Patient and loving God, help me to be patient enough to see the big picture, and teach me restraint, not to speak or act from emotion before I understand the situation and discern your will. Amen.

TAKING THINGS INTO YOUR OWN HANDS

From the Rule

Every occasion of presumption shall be avoided in the monastery, and we decree that no one be allowed to excommunicate or to strike any of his brethren unless the Abbot has given him the authority. Those who offend in this matter shall be rebuked in the presence of all, that the rest may have fear.

But children up to 15 years of age shall be carefully controlled and watched by all, yet this too with all moderation and discretion. All, therefore, who presume without the Abbot's instructions to punish those above that age or who lose their temper with them, shall undergo the discipline of the Rule; for it is written, "Do not to another what you would not want done to yourself" (Tob. 4:15). (Chapter 70)

Matthew 7

Do not judge, so that you may not be judged. [2] For with the judgment you make you will be judged, and the measure you give will be the measure you get. [3] Why do you see the speck in your neighbor's eye, but do not notice the log in your own eye? [4] Or how can you say to your neighbor, "Let me take the speck out of your eye," while the log is in your own eye? [5] You hypocrite, first take the log out of your own eye, and then you will see clearly to take the speck out of your neighbor's eye. . . .
   [12] In everything do to others as you would have them do to you; for this is the law and the prophets.

Contemplation

1. What word, phrase, or image from either of the two passages resonates with you?
2. What connection can you make to your own life?
3. What might God be calling you to do?

Reflection

Where does this come from, this tendency of people to want to punish others of whom they disapprove? It seems to be the dark side of human nature: road rage, hate crimes, physical abuse of children. Perhaps it comes from one's frustration with living in an imperfect world. Some people punish to gain control, to feel more powerful themselves. And often, the things that drive us most crazy about another person are those characteristics we secretly know to be true about ourselves, seeing the speck in your neighbor's eye while in denial about the log in your own eye.

   Benedict understood these tendencies and realized the danger they present to peace in the community. An environment in which everyone took discipline into their own hands would create uproar and chaos. Discipline clearly needs to remain in the hands of the abbot.

   However, Benedict also understood that "it takes a village to raise a child," and that many watchful eyes were necessary to shepherd the younger charges along the road to maturity. But here, as he does so many times in the Rule, he cautions moderation and discretion, understanding that children and youth need a positive and affirming environment in which to flourish. He sums it all up in the reciprocal version of what we know as the Golden Rule: *Don't do to another what you would not want done to yourself.*

Prayer

Patient and loving God, teach me the self-awareness to rein in my anger and withhold judgment on my brothers and sisters. Help me to respond in love, as you have shown abundant love to me. Amen.

THE DISCIPLINE OF CHILDREN

From the Rule

Every age and degree of understanding should have its proper measure of discipline. With regard to boys and adolescents, therefore, or those who cannot understand the seriousness of the penalty of excommunication, whenever such as these are delinquent let them be subjected to severe fasts or brought to terms by harsh beatings, that they may be cured. (Chapter 30)

Proverbs 13

[24] Those who spare the rod hate their children, but those who love them are diligent to discipline them.

and Luke 18

[15] People were bringing even infants to him that he might touch them; and when the disciples saw it, they sternly ordered them not to do it. [16] But Jesus called for them and said, "Let the little children come to me, and do not stop them; for it is to such as these that the kingdom of God belongs. [17] Truly I tell you, whoever does not receive the kingdom of God as a little child will never enter it."

Contemplation

1. What word, phrase, or image from these passages resonates with you?
2. What connection can you make to your own life?
3. What might God be calling you to do?

Reflection

In Benedict's time (end of the fifth, beginning of the sixth century), it was common for people to dedicate their children to religious upbringing within the monastery. Patricians and senators of Rome offered their sons to become monks under Benedict's care. Wealthy families knew that their young men would be educated and become literate. The poor knew their sons would be clothed, fed, and taken care of. The older monks, who had chosen to forego wives and families for the quiet life of a monastic, must have sometimes been at a loss knowing how to manage rambunctious and impetuous youngsters.

This chapter has to be taken in its historical context. Corporal punishment was the norm at the time. "Spare the rod and spoil the child." The text was written centuries before child psychology, and as true of many parents today, monks probably disciplined as they had been disciplined while growing up. Joan Chittister reminds us that corporal punishment was practiced in American homes and schools until the late twentieth century.[4]

Judgment of Benedict's advice on child discipline also needs to be tempered with other places in the Rule where he seems downright indulgent. In chapter 37 he advocates compassion for the young and "kindly consideration," not requiring them, for example, to follow the same strict dietary restrictions imposed on the older monks.

Prayer

Blessed Lord, thank you for the love you showed to everyone, and especially to children. Help me to remember that the kingdom of heaven belongs to children whom Jesus loved. Amen.

WELCOMING BACK

From the Rule

If a brother who through his own fault leaves the monastery should wish to return, let him first promise full reparation for his having gone away; and then let him be received in the lowest place, as a test of his humility. And if he should leave again, let him be taken back again, and so a third time; but he should understand that after this all way of return is denied him. (Chapter 29)

---

4. Chittister, *Rule of Benedict*, 103.

Luke 15

²⁵ Now his elder son was in the field; and when he came and approached the house, he heard music and dancing. ²⁶ He called one of the slaves and asked what was going on. ²⁷ He replied, "Your brother has come, and your father has killed the fatted calf, because he has got him back safe and sound." ²⁸ Then he became angry and refused to go in. His father came out and began to plead with him. ²⁹ But he answered his father, "Listen! For all these years I have been working like a slave for you, and I have never disobeyed your command; yet you have never given me even a young goat so that I might celebrate with my friends. ³⁰ But when this son of yours came back, who has devoured your property with prostitutes, you killed the fatted calf for him!" ³¹ Then the father said to him, "Son, you are always with me, and all that is mine is yours. ³² But we had to celebrate and rejoice, because this brother of yours was dead and has come to life; he was lost and has been found."

Contemplation

1. What word, phrase, or image from either of the two passages resonates with you?
2. What connection can you make to your own life?
3. What might God be calling you to do?

Reflection

Benedict instructs us to welcome back the rebellious member of the community who repents and returns—even as many as three times! This chapter reminds me of the parable of the prodigal son in the Gospel of Luke.

The sentiments of the forgiving abbot may not be aligned with the attitudes of the other brothers or sisters whom the departed one has abandoned and wronged. This normal response is reflected as well in the parable in Luke's Gospel, in which the faithful, reliable brother who has remained and worked isn't thrilled to see all the fuss made at the return of his profligate brother. And by the second or third return, cynicism may well increase as any sympathy the others may have had wears thin. It is probably for this reason Benedict advises that the prodigal's repentance and humility should be tested by giving him the last place in the pecking order.

It will be a test of our humility to keep these emotions in check and, with true love, welcome back to the community the one who was lost to us.

Prayer

Merciful Father, just as you told your disciples to forgive their brother or sister not seven times, but seventy-seven times, give me the humility and charity always to welcome back into fellowship my brothers and sisters. Amen.

9

PRACTICAL CONCERNS

FASHION FOLLOWS FUNCTION

From the Rule

Let clothing be given to the brethren according to the nature of the place in which they dwell and its climate; for in cold regions more will be needed, and in warm regions less. This is to be taken into consideration, therefore, by the Abbot. We believe, however, that in ordinary places the following dress is sufficient for each monk: a tunic, a cowl (thick and woolly for winter, thin or worn for summer), a scapular for work, stockings and shoes to cover the feet.

The monks should not complain about the color or the coarseness of any of these things, but be content with what can be found in the district where they live and can be purchased cheaply. The Abbot shall see to the size of the garments, that they be not too short for those who wear them, but of the proper fit.

Let those who receive new clothes always give back the old ones at once, to be put away in the wardrobe for the poor. For it is sufficient if a monk has two tunics and two cowls, to allow for night wear and for the washing of these garments; more than that is superfluity and should be taken away. Let them return their stockings also and anything else that is old when they receive new ones.

Those who are sent on a journey shall receive drawers from the wardrobe, which they shall wash and restore on their return. And let their cowls and tunics be somewhat better than what they usually wear. These they shall receive from the wardrobe when they set out on a journey, and restore when they return. (Chapter 55, Part 1)

Luke 12

22 He said to his disciples, "Therefore I tell you, do not worry about your life, what you will eat, or about your body, what you will wear. 23 For life is more than food, and the body more than clothing. 24 Consider the ravens: they neither sow nor reap, they have neither storehouse nor barn, and yet God feeds them. Of how much more

value are you than the birds! [25] And can any of you by worrying add a single hour to your span of life? [26] If then you are not able to do so small a thing as that, why do you worry about the rest? [27] Consider the lilies, how they grow: they neither toil nor spin; yet I tell you, even Solomon in all his glory was not clothed like one of these. [28] But if God so clothes the grass of the field, which is alive today and tomorrow is thrown into the oven, how much more will he clothe you—you of little faith!"

Contemplation

1. What word, phrase, or image from either of the two passages resonates with you?
2. What connection can you make to your own life?
3. What might God be calling you to do?

Reflection

I've been told that the first rule of design is "form follows function." The maxim was actually coined by a modernist architect, Louis Sullivan, who implied that ornament was not the primary goal of good design, but should only be used judiciously. Practical spaces, he said, should be spare and crisp in their appearance (although Sullivan was not above using lush art nouveau and Celtic revival decoration to break up plain surfaces).

In Benedict's aesthetic, the rule could apply to clothing as well. In the work they had to do around the monastery, monks needed a tunic, a warm, wooly cowl, a scapular (a loose outer garment that hung from the shoulders), socks and shoes. Benedict does not mention items such as belts, brooches, buckles, leggings, or rings. While he dismisses ornamentation, he does insist on warmth and proper fit. He allowed for attractive apparel in his recommendation that those sent on a journey should wear something presentable, "somewhat better than what they usually wear."

The conversation about clothing continues the discouragement of pride in personal belongings begun in chapter 54 of the Rule. Do modern Benedictines show a similar disregard for ornamentation and fashion? I confess that I do not. Most of us like to look nice. But we should keep in mind that spending excessive time in clothing stores or online catalogs is not usually the best use of our time. Our whole-hearted priority should be on building the kingdom of heaven.

Prayer

Patient God, who must look on his creatures with indulgent humor, forgive us for being distracted by the unimportant things of life. Let me not preoccupy myself with the things that have no eternal significance. Amen.

ALL THAT ONE NEEDS

From the Rule

For bedding let this suffice: a mattress, a blanket, a coverlet and a pillow. The beds, moreover, are to be examined frequently by the Abbot, to see if any private property be found in them. If anyone should be found to have something that he did not receive from the Abbot, let him undergo the most severe discipline.

And in order that this vice of private ownership may be cut out by the roots, the Abbot should provide all the necessary articles: cowl, tunic, stockings, shoes, belt, knife, stylus, needle, handkerchief, writing tablets; that all pretext of need may be taken away. Yet the Abbot should always keep in mind the sentence from the Acts of the Apostles that "distribution was made to each according as anyone had need" (Acts 4:35). In this manner, therefore, let the Abbot consider weaknesses of the needy and not the ill-will of the envious. But in all his decisions let him think about the retribution of God. (Chapter 55, Part 2)

Acts 4

[32] Now the whole group of those who believed were of one heart and soul, and no one claimed private ownership of any possessions, but everything they owned was held in common. [33] With great power the apostles gave their testimony to the resurrection of the Lord Jesus, and great grace was upon them all. [34] There was not a needy person among them, for as many as owned lands or houses sold them and brought the proceeds of what was sold.

Contemplation

1. What word, phrase, or image from either of the two passages resonates with you?
2. What connection can you make to your own life?
3. What might God be calling you to do?

Reflection

One could describe the arc of one's life as years of wanting more followed by years of wanting less. As children, we want more toys, more crayons, more ice cream, more attention from the adults in our life. As adolescents we want more friends, nicer clothes, a car, and more hours in the day to stay up and have fun. And adulthood brings its own new categories of more: a more prestigious job, a nicer house, a high-performance car, and first-class tickets.

However, at a certain time in our life we desire less. We discover that our possessions have a way of owning us. We pare down our needs to fewer things. My husband and I moved to a new condo to have less lawn to mow and fewer rooms to take care of. And although we did considerable purging before our move, I still walk into our basement and am overwhelmed by the art we have no room to hang, Christmas decorations far too many for our tree, and the boxes of things we still haven't opened after our last move.

Benedict's idea of being given simple, basic necessities is an appealing one. A cowl, tunic, stockings, shoes, belt—how difficult would it be to decide what to wear each morning? And your knife, stylus, needle, and writing tablet would be no better or worse than anyone else's. If your life is dedicated to prayer and contemplation, what time would you have to worry about the physical things that are already provided for you? This simplicity of life is suited to one simple mission in life: to love God and serve others.

Prayer

Gracious and generous God who attends to all our needs, help my single focus to be on you. Let me want nothing but you and the building of your kingdom. Amen.

ACCOMMODATION AND MODERATION

From the Rule

We think it sufficient for the daily dinner, whether at the sixth or the ninth hour, that every table have two cooked dishes on account of individual infirmities, so that he who for some reason cannot eat of the one may make his meal of the other. Therefore, let two cooked dishes suffice for all the brethren; and if any fruit or fresh vegetables are available, let a third dish be added.

Let a good pound weight of bread suffice for the day, whether there be only one meal or both dinner and supper. If they are to have supper, the cellarer shall reserve a third of that pound, to be given them at supper.

But if it happens that the work was heavier, it shall lie within the Abbot's discretion and power, should it be expedient, to add something to the fare. Above all things, however, over-indulgence must be avoided and a monk must never be overtaken by indigestion; for there is nothing so opposed to the Christian character as over-indulgence according to Our Lord's words, "See to it that your hearts be not burdened with over-indulgence" (Luke 21:34).

Young boys shall not receive the same amount of food as their elders, but less; and frugality shall be observed in all circumstances.

Except the sick who are very weak, let all abstain entirely from eating the flesh of four-footed animals. (Chapter 39)

Luke 21

34 Be on guard so that your hearts are not weighed down with dissipation and drunkenness and the worries of this life, and that day does not catch you unexpectedly, 35 like a trap. For it will come upon all who live on the face of the whole earth. 36 Be alert at all times, praying that you may have the strength to escape all these things that will take place, and to stand before the Son of Man.

and Matthew 6

25 Therefore I tell you, do not worry about your life, what you will eat or what you will drink, or about your body, what you will wear. Is not life more than food, and the body more than clothing? 26 Look at the birds of the air; they neither sow nor reap nor gather into barns, and yet your heavenly Father feeds them. Are you not of more value than they?

Contemplation

1. What word, phrase, or image from these passages resonates with you?
2. What connection can you make to your own life?
3. What might God be calling you to do?

Reflection

Food allergies, vegan diets, and celiac disease are some of the issues that my Benedictine group has to deal with in planning our monthly community meal. Fortunately, Benedict gave us a rule about accommodating "individual infirmities" related to food: prepare two dishes, one of which everyone can eat regardless of their food sensitivities. And, when you can, supplement it with plenty of bread and fresh fruits and vegetables. Accommodation is also made for the manual worker who may need a few more carbohydrates to get them through the day.

Accommodation is balanced by moderation. "Over-indulgence must be avoided." The big point is that we shouldn't have to worry about what we eat. Preoccupation with having enough or with what we can or cannot eat shouldn't distract us from our more important pursuits: prayer and service. As the writer of

Matthew's gospel tells us, "Look at the birds of the air; they neither sow nor reap nor gather into barns, and yet your heavenly Father feeds them. Are you not of more value than they?"

Prayer

Heavenly Provider, I am grateful that you look out for my needs. Keep me mindful of the needs of others, so that those I serve also will not worry about your providence. Amen.

DRINKING IN MODERATION

From the Rule

"Everyone has his own gift from God, one in this way and another in that" (1 Cor. 7:7). It is therefore with some misgiving that we regulate the measure of others' sustenance. Nevertheless, keeping in view the needs of the weak, we believe that a half bottle of wine a day is sufficient for each. But those to whom God gives the strength to abstain should know that they will receive a special reward.

If the circumstances of the place, or the work or the heat of summer require a greater measure, the superior shall use her judgment in the matter, taking care always that there be no occasion for surfeit or drunkenness. We read it is true, that wine is by no means a drink for monastics; but since the monastics of our day cannot be persuaded of this let us at least agree to drink sparingly and not to satiety, because "wine makes even the wise fall away" (Eccles. 19:2).

But where the circumstances of the place are such that not even the measure prescribed above can be supplied, but much less or none at all, let those who live there bless God and not murmur. Above all things do we give this admonition, that they abstain from murmuring. (Chapter 40)

Ephesians 5

[15] Be careful then how you live, not as unwise people but as wise, [16] making the most of the time, because the days are evil. [17] So do not be foolish, but understand what the will of the Lord is. [18] Do not get drunk with wine, for that is debauchery; but be filled with the Spirit, [19] as you sing psalms and hymns and spiritual songs among yourselves, singing and making melody to the Lord in your hearts, [20] giving thanks to God the Father at all times and for everything in the name of our Lord Jesus Christ.

Contemplation

1. What word, phrase, or image from either of the two passages resonates with you?
2. What connection can you make to your own life?
3. What might God be calling you to do?

Reflection

Benedict, for all his wisdom, sometimes takes scripture out of context. Both of his scriptural citations, one from 1 Corinthians and the other from Ecclesiasticus (Sirach), actually address sexual immorality. The Ecclesiasticus reference actually says "Wine *and women* lead intelligent men astray." But Benedict can be forgiven for this liberty because I'm sure that in his day, as in ours, excessive drink is sometimes a factor in sexual indiscretion.

And his advice is wise in that moderation in wine is a theme throughout the Bible, as in the passage above from Ephesians and several other scriptures in the Epistles. I am conscious of the effect of a glass or two of wine during the day on my energy and productivity, and I try to be sensitive about my alcohol consumption around friends who do not drink because of addiction issues. Again, we should be clear-eyed in our focus on being Christ's hands and feet in the world, and we should shun anything that compromises our ability to do God's work.

Prayer

God of wisdom, thank you for all the good things in life. Teach me the importance of moderation so that I will ever be alert and prepared to serve you. Amen.

GLADDENING AND STRENGTHENING

From the Rule

From holy Easter until Pentecost let the brothers take dinner at the sixth hour and supper in the evening. From Pentecost throughout the summer, unless the monks have work in the fields, let them fast on Wednesdays and Fridays until the ninth hour; on the other days let them dine at the sixth hour. This dinner at the sixth hour shall be the daily schedule if they have work in the fields or the heat of summer is extreme; the Abbot's foresight shall decide on this. Thus it is that he should adapt and arrange everything in such a way that souls may be saved and that the brethren may do their work without just cause for murmuring.

From the Ides of September until the beginning of Lent let them always take their dinner at the ninth hour. In Lent until Easter let them dine in the evening. But this evening hour shall be so determined that they will not need the light of a lamp while eating. Indeed at all seasons let the hour, whether for supper or for dinner, be so arranged that everything will be done by daylight. (Chapter 41)

Psalm 104

13 From your lofty abode you water the mountains;
   the earth is satisfied with the fruit of your work.
14 You cause the grass to grow for the cattle,
   and plants for people to use,
   to bring forth food from the earth,
15 and wine to gladden the human heart,
   oil to make the face shine,
   and bread to strengthen the human heart. . . .
27 These all look to you
   to give them their food in due season;
28 when you give to them, they gather it up;
   when you open your hand, they are filled with good things.

Contemplation

1. What word, phrase, or image from either of the two passages resonates with you?
2. What connection can you make to your own life?
3. What might God be calling you to do?

Reflection

In Benedict's time, the counting of the hours of the day began at sunrise, so the first hour of the day began at about six thirty in the morning. As it is today, the monastery's main meal of day was the midday meal at about twelve thirty, or the sixth hour. It appears from this chapter that the monks had two meals a day, a midday meal and an evening supper. It also seems that the monks fasted on Wednesdays and Fridays, only taking one meal at about three thirty (the ninth hour), *except* if they had work in the fields or the heat was extreme. The eating schedule was different from mid-September until Lent. The abbot had discretion over when to schedule meals as long as they took place during daylight.

As everywhere in the Rule, sensitivity and moderation is preeminent. The norm is disciplined restraint, but with a good measure of grace. Benedict says that everything should be done "in such a way that souls may be saved and that the brethren may do their work without just cause for murmuring." Meals should reflect God's bounty and providence. The monks look to God "to give them their food in due season." As the psalm tells us, food and wine gladden and strengthen the heart.

Prayer

Blessed are you, gracious God, for giving us food and drink to sustain our lives and gladden our hearts. Amen.

During a Silent Meal

From the Rule

The meals of the brethren should not be without reading. Nor should the reader be anyone who happens to take up the book; but there should be a reader for the whole week, entering that office on Sunday. Let this incoming reader, after Mass and Communion, ask all to pray for him that God may keep him from the spirit of pride. And let him intone the following verse, which shall be said three times by all in the oratory: "O Lord, open my lips, and my mouth shall declare Your praise." Then, having received a blessing, let him enter on the reading.

And let absolute silence be kept at table, so that no whispering may be heard nor any voice except the reader's. As to the things they need while they eat and drink, let the brethren pass them to one another so that no one need ask for anything. If anything is needed, however, let it be asked for by means of some audible sign rather than by speech. Nor shall anyone at table presume to ask questions about the reading or anything else, lest that give occasion for talking; except that the Superior may perhaps wish to say something briefly for the purpose of edification.

The brother who is reader for the week shall take a little refreshment before he begins to read, on account of the Holy Communion and lest perhaps the fast be hard for him to bear. He shall take his meal afterwards with the kitchen and table servers of the week.

The brethren are not to read or chant in order, but only those who edify their hearers. (Chapter 38)

Psalm 51

¹⁰ Create in me a clean heart, O God,
and put a new and right spirit within me.

¹¹ Do not cast me away from your presence,
and do not take your holy spirit from me.

¹² Restore to me the joy of your salvation,
and sustain in me a willing spirit.

¹³ Then I will teach transgressors your ways,
and sinners will return to you. . . .

¹⁵ O Lord, open my lips,
and my mouth will declare your praise.

¹⁶ For you have no delight in sacrifice;
if I were to give a burnt-offering, you would not be pleased.

¹⁷ The sacrifice acceptable to God is a broken spirit;
a broken and contrite heart, O God, you will not despise.

Contemplation

1. What word, phrase, or image from either of the two passages resonates with you?
2. What connection can you make to your own life?
3. What might God be calling you to do?

Reflection

At the Monastery of Christ in the Desert, following the Rule, no conversation takes place at the meals. At the midday meal on my first visit, after two chanted prayers, monks and guests sat to hear the first reading, a short passage from Exodus. Then, as the meal was served, the designated reader for the week began the second reading from a devotional book with chapters on compassion, forgiveness, anger, and humility. On other visits, the reader has read from biographies of modern saints. At the end of the meal, the reader read a short passage from the lives of the early fathers. Lunch ended with a chanted thanksgiving and a sung prayer to Saint Benedict.

This chapter on the meal readings underscores several principles of the Rule. The first principle follows Benedict's teaching on restraint of speech: during meals, complete silence. The introvert in me found great relief in not having to make dinner table conversation with the strangers on either side of me. I was free just to sit in silence and listen. The second principle is humility; the reader asks for prayer to shield him from "the spirit of vanity" and waits to take his meal with the kitchen workers and servers after others have left. A third theme addresses mutual obedience: the brothers being sensitive enough to one another's needs as they eat and drink, so that no one needs to ask for anything. Mealtime, it seems, is a perfect time to practice holy silence, humility, and service.

Prayer

Patient God, help me in every moment of my life, even during meals, to be obedient to you, looking for opportunities to listen and serve with humility. Amen.

THE SIGNIFICANCE OF A MEAL

From the Rule

Anyone who does not come to table before the verse, so that all together may say the verse and the oration and all sit down to table at the same time—anyone who through his own carelessness or bad habit does not come on time shall be corrected for this up to the second time. If then he does not amend, he shall not be allowed to share in the common table, but shall be separated from the company of all and made to eat alone, and his portion of wine shall be taken away from him, until he has made satisfaction and has amended. And let him suffer a like penalty who is not present at the verse said after the meal. But if anyone is offered something by the Superior and refuses to take it, then when the time comes that he desires what he formerly refused or something else, let him receive nothing whatever until he has made proper satisfaction. (Chapter 43, Part 2)

Luke 14

[16] Then Jesus said to him, "Someone gave a great dinner and invited many. [17] At the time for the dinner he sent his slave to say to those who had been invited, 'Come; for everything is ready now.' [18] But they all alike began to make excuses. The first said to him, 'I have bought a piece of land, and I must go out and see it; please accept my regrets.' [19] Another said, 'I have bought five yoke of oxen, and I am going to try them out; please accept my regrets.' [20] Another said, 'I have just been married, and therefore I cannot come.' [21] So the slave returned and reported this to his master. Then the owner of the house became angry and said to his slave, 'Go out at once into the streets and lanes of the town and bring in the poor, the crippled, the blind, and the lame.' [22] And the slave said, 'Sir, what you ordered has been done, and there is still room.' [23] Then the master said to the slave, 'Go out into the roads and lanes, and compel people to come in, so

that my house may be filled. [24] For I tell you, none of those who were invited will taste my dinner.'"

Contemplation

1. What word, phrase, or image from either of the two passages resonates with you?
2. What connection can you make to your own life?
3. What might God be calling you to do?

Reflection

I love being invited to dinner with friends. One cannot overlook the significance of eating together to strengthen relationships and create community. Jesus fed people and shared meals with his disciples and followers. The parable in Luke (above) reveals the significance of an invitation to table and the seriousness of ignoring that opportunity for fellowship.

In my occasional visits to the monastery, meals were important gathering times. Even though the meal was eaten in silence, the monks did have a ritual that underscored the importance and sacredness of the meal. Monks and guests entered together, prayed and chanted together, listened and learned together as the lector read from the early fathers or contemporary devotional books. Once, when I came late to a meal, I had to wait outside the refectory until the others were finished but was allowed to eat with the kitchen workers afterward. (A very gracious monk kept me company during my wait.)

In our own secular life, meals are an incredible time for relationship-building. That's why we have friends over for dinner or meet people at a café for lunch. I always feel I've gotten to know someone so much better after sharing a meal with them, especially when that common meal takes place in one of our homes. Meals are often the occasion when we stop during the day to thank God for the blessings given us. They can be sacramental occasions.

And so, being on time to a meal is as important as being on time to worship. We are honoring God and each other by making prompt attendance a priority.

Prayer

Gracious and generous God, who gives us food and friends and fellowship to sustain our lives and make our hearts glad, help me to acknowledge and respect those times when I can have a meal with others. Amen.

SACRED SLEEP

From the Rule

Let each one sleep in a separate bed. Let them receive bedding suitable to their manner of life, according to the Abbot's directions. If possible let all sleep in one place; but if the number does not allow this, let them take their rest by tens or twenties with the seniors who have charge of them. A candle shall be kept burning in the room until morning.

Let the monks sleep clothed and girded with belts or cords—but not with their knives at their sides, lest they cut themselves in their sleep—and thus be always ready to rise without delay when the signal is given and hasten to be before one another at the Work of God, yet with all gravity and decorum.

The younger brethren shall not have beds next to one another, but among those of the older ones. When they rise for the Work of God, let them gently encourage one another, that the drowsy may have no excuse. (Chapter 22)

Psalm 4

1 Answer me when I call, O God of my right!
 You gave me room when I was in distress.
 Be gracious to me, and hear my prayer.
2 How long, you people, shall my honor suffer shame?
 How long will you love vain words, and seek after lies? *Selah*
3 But know that the LORD has set apart the faithful for himself;
 the LORD hears when I call to him.
4 When you are disturbed,[a] do not sin;
 ponder it on your beds, and be silent. *Selah*
5 Offer right sacrifices,
 and put your trust in the LORD.
6 There are many who say, "O that we might see some good!
 Let the light of your face shine on us, O LORD!"
7 You have put gladness in my heart
 more than when their grain and wine abound.
8 I will both lie down and sleep in peace;
 for you alone, O LORD, make me lie down in safety.

Contemplation

1. What word, phrase, or image from either of the two passages resonates with you?
2. What connection can you make to your own life?
3. What might God be calling you to do?

Reflection

To *ora et labora*, prayer and work, Benedict implicitly adds another important part of monastic life: sleep! Sleep is an important part of everyone's life. As William Blake said, "Think in the morning. Act in the noon. Eat in the evening. Sleep in the night." Sleep enables us to have the cognitive abilities to do the work we have to do throughout the day. The way you feel during waking hours depends on what happens while you're sleeping. During sleep, your body is working to support brain function and overall health. While you are sleeping, your brain is preparing for the next day.

So devoting a chapter to sleep, as Benedict did, is not a trivial thing. He does so knowing that sleep is also a sacred part of life. Preparing to sleep is an important time to take stock of your life before God. As Psalm 4 says, "ponder it on your beds, and be silent." It is a time of reassurance, remembering God's grace. "I will both lie down and sleep in peace; for you alone, O LORD, make me lie down in safety."

Prayer

Loving God, let me turn my thoughts toward you before I go to sleep. Watch over me as I sleep that I may rise refreshed and ready to serve you with new energy and commitment. Amen.

A SACRED PLACE

From the Rule

Let the oratory be what it is called, a place of prayer; and let nothing else be done there or kept there. When the Work of God is ended, let all go out in perfect silence, and let reverence for God be observed, so that any sister who may wish to pray privately will not be hindered by another's misconduct. And at other times also, if anyone should want to pray by herself, let her go in simply and pray, not in a loud voice but with tears and fervor of heart. She who does not say her prayers in this way, therefore, shall not be permitted to remain in the oratory when the Work of God is ended, lest another be hindered, as we have said. (Chapter 52)

1 Kings 8

[27] But will God indeed dwell on the earth? Even heaven and the highest heaven cannot contain you, much less this house that I have built! [28] Regard your servant's prayer and his plea, O LORD my God, heeding the cry and the prayer that your servant prays to you today; [29] that your eyes may be open night and day toward this house, the place of which you said, "My name shall be there," that you may heed the prayer that your servant prays toward this place. [30] Hear the plea of your servant and of your people Israel when they pray toward this place; O hear in heaven your dwelling place; heed and forgive.

Contemplation

1. What word, phrase, or image from either of the two passages resonates with you?
2. What connection can you make to your own life?
3. What might God be calling you to do?

Reflection

God is present everywhere: on mountaintops, in majestic canyons, in squalid villages, and in back alleys. However, there is something to be said for sacred spaces, rooms or sanctuaries specifically set aside as places to meet God. The place is often set apart, immaculately clean, quiet, and comfortable. It may have art that turns our thoughts toward God, candles, religious objects, and stained-glass windows. You might notice that when a person enters such a place, they will stop conversation or lower their voice almost to a whisper, even though no one tells them to do so, because the space itself signals the need for reverence. Joan Chittister wrote, "There is . . . such a thing as a spiritual well where simply being in that place can tap open that special part of our souls and enable us to touch the sacred in the secular."[1] Benedict clearly sees the importance of such a place and makes it clear that this space should be set aside for prayer and for no other purpose.

Prayer

Ever-present God, let me look for you in the workplace or the shops or on the street, but thank you also for the secluded, quiet places where I can still my mind as I enjoy your presence. Amen.

---

1. Chittister, *Rule of Benedict*, 139.

ATTENTION TO LITTLE THINGS

From the Rule

For the care of the monastery's property in tools, clothing and other articles let the Abbot appoint brethren on whose manner of life and character he can rely; and let him, as he shall judge to be expedient, consign the various articles to them, to be looked after and to be collected again. The Abbot shall keep a list of these articles, so that as the brethren succeed one another in their assignments he may know what he gives and what he receives back. If anyone treats the monastery's property in a slovenly or careless way, let him be corrected. If he fails to amend, let him undergo the discipline of the Rule. (Chapter 32)

Luke 12

[42] And the Lord said, "Who then is the faithful and prudent manager whom his master will put in charge of his slaves, to give them their allowance of food at the proper time? [43] Blessed is that slave whom his master will find at work when he arrives. [44] Truly I tell you, he will put that one in charge of all his possessions. [45] But if that slave says to himself, 'My master is delayed in coming,' and if he begins to beat the other slaves, men and women, and to eat and drink and get drunk, [46] the master of that slave will come on a day when he does not expect him and at an hour that he does not know, and will cut him in pieces, and put him with the unfaithful. . . . [48] From everyone to whom much has been given, much will be required; and from the one to whom much has been entrusted, even more will be demanded."

Contemplation

1. What word, phrase, or image from either of the two passages resonates with you?
2. What connection can you make to your own life?
3. What might God be calling you to do?

Reflection

In a monastic setting, the work of the brothers and sisters is prayer (*opus dei*). Taking care of their home, the monastery, is also sacred work (*ora et labora*). In order to devote attention to important things, the little things in life have to be taken care of as well. Tools must be where we need them. Materials must be in ready supply. All the various articles of work must be cared for. Using something that is in poor shape or not being able to find the tool or material we need is a time-wasting distraction that creates an obstacle to completing our important tasks.

Benedict clearly does not promote materialism in his Rule, as we see when he addresses private property, but neither does he teach *anti*materialism. Tools, supplies, and food are all important to the life of the community.

I've often been aware that the principle applies well to my own life. Disorder in my work space, lack of attention to what's in my cupboard or refrigerator, or neglecting small but important household tasks all keep me from making good use of my time and have a detrimental effect on my sense of well-being. Neglecting my times of prayer, as inconsequential as they may seem at the time, affects my spiritual well-being. Attending to the little things, material and spiritual, benefits me in many ways.

Prayer

Master of all, give me the wisdom and discipline to attend to the little things, so that I can be a faithful servant in the work you have given me to do. Amen.

BEING AWAY

From the Rule

Those brethren who are working at a great distance and cannot get to the oratory at the proper time—the Abbot judging that such is the case—shall perform the Work of God in the place where they are working, bending their knees in reverence before God.

Likewise those who have been sent on a journey shall not let the appointed Hours pass by, but shall say the Office by themselves as well as they can, and not neglect to render the task of their service. (Chapter 50)

Luke 10

After this the Lord appointed seventy others and sent them on ahead of him in pairs to every town and place where he himself intended to go. ² He said to them, "The harvest is plentiful, but the laborers are few; therefore ask the Lord of the harvest to send out laborers into his harvest. ³ Go on your way. See, I am sending you out like lambs into the midst of wolves. ⁴ Carry no purse, no bag, no sandals; and greet no one on the road. ⁵ Whatever house you enter, first say, 'Peace to this house!' ⁶ And if anyone is there who shares in peace, your peace will rest on that person; but if not, it will return to you. [7] Remain in the same house, eating and drinking whatever they provide, for the laborer deserves to be paid. Do not move about from house to house. [8] Whenever you enter a town and its people welcome you, eat what is set before you; [9] cure the sick who are there, and say to them, 'The kingdom of God has come near to you.'"

Contemplation

1. What word, phrase, or image from either of the two passages resonates with you?
2. What connection can you make to your own life?
3. What might God be calling you to do?

Reflection

Benedict drew a sharp distinction between monastic life and life in the outside world. As far as possible, each of his monasteries formed an independent, self-supporting community where monks had little need of going outside its walls for anything. Monastery culture was a life devoted primarily to prayer. While prayer remains a priority in monastic settings, monasteries today are also often devoted to service in their communities. Helping out in a local church, participating in a youth program, managing a day shelter, or simply going into town for supplies may take the monk out of the monastery for an afternoon, a day, or possibly longer.

It is good to remember that Jesus sent out his followers to preach the gospel to those in surrounding areas. However, the *opus dei*—prayer—must continue, and Benedict instructs his ambassadors to kneel and pray "as best they can" while they are away.

Traveling is the most challenging time for me to keep my daily prayer practice. Different schedules and the constant presence of traveling partners make it difficult to keep to one's usual routine. I must keep in my consciousness that communication with God needs to happen every day, and that, like the monks, prayer is the most important thing I do.

Prayer

Patient God, in whose presence I am always welcome, help me never to forget my time with you and its importance to my relationship to you and the work of your kingdom. Amen.

EATING OUT

From the Rule

A Brother who is sent out on some business and is expected to return to the monastery that same day shall not presume to eat while he is out, even if he is urgently requested to do so by any person whomsoever, unless he has permission from his Abbot. And if he acts otherwise, let him be excommunicated. (Chapter 51)

Romans 14

[19] Let us then pursue what makes for peace and for mutual upbuilding. [20] Do not, for the sake of food, destroy the work of God. Everything is indeed clean, but it is wrong for you to make others fall by what you eat; [21] it is good not to eat meat or drink wine or do anything that makes your brother or sister stumble. [22] The faith that you have, have as your own conviction before God. Blessed are those who have no reason to condemn themselves because of what they approve. [23] But those who have doubts are condemned if they eat, because they do not act from faith; for whatever does not proceed from faith is sin.

Contemplation

1. What word, phrase, or image from either of the two passages resonates with you?
2. What connection can you make to your own life?
3. What might God be calling you to do?

Reflection

This chapter of the Rule is one of the hardest to understand. What was wrong about accepting the hospitality of someone the monk might meet in his travels outside the monastery? Was food safety an issue? Perhaps the food prepared in strange kitchens wasn't always in keeping with hygienic standards or follow the dietary guidelines of the Rule. Was the food too rich and spoil the appetite the traveling monk would have for the much simpler monastery fare? Did dining with strangers lead to too much wine consumption? Or was it simply that something more important awaited the monk back at the monastery and dining with a new friend took time away from the work of prayer?

In his commentary,[2] G. A. Simon cautions oblates against living like *bon vivants*, reminding them that they have chosen God as their portion. This is a

---

2. Simon, *Commentary for Benedictine Oblates*, 378.

reminder to me that, in spite of my attraction to elegant parties, gourmet dining, and fine wine, I am called to live simply. I should be thoughtful about how I spend my time and mindful of those who have little. As Benedict reminds us in chapter 49, the life of a monk ought to have about it the character of a Lenten observance.

Prayer

Munificent God, help me always to be obedient to you, mindful of what I eat and drink, and quick to return to the work you have called me to do. Amen.

TRAVEL STORIES

From the Rule

Let brethren who are sent on a journey commend themselves to the prayers of all the brethren and of the Abbot; and always at the last prayer of the Work of God let a prayer be made for all absent brethren.

When brethren return from a journey, at the end of each canonical hour of the Work of God on the day they return, let them lie prostrate on the floor of the oratory and beg the prayers of all on account of any faults that may have caught them off guard on the road, through the seeing or hearing of something evil, or through idle talk. And let no one presume to tell another whatever he may have seen or heard outside of the monastery, because this causes very great harm. But if anyone presumes to do so, let him undergo the punishment of the Rule. And let him be punished likewise who would presume to leave the enclosure of the monastery and go anywhere or do anything, however small, without an order from the Abbot. (Chapter 67)

John 17

[11] And now I am no longer in the world, but they are in the world, and I am coming to you. Holy Father, protect them in your name that you have given me, so that they may be one, as we are one. [12] While I was with them, I protected them in your name that you have given me. I guarded them, and not one of them was lost except the one destined to be lost, so that the scripture might be fulfilled. [13] But now I am coming to you, and I speak these things in the world so that they may have my joy made complete in themselves. [14] I have given them your word, and the world has hated them because they do not belong to the world, just as I do not belong to the world. [15] I am not asking you to take them out of the world, but I ask you to protect them from the evil one. [16] They do not belong to the world, just as I do not

belong to the world. ¹⁷ Sanctify them in the truth; your word is truth. ¹⁸ As you have sent me into the world, so I have sent them into the world. ¹⁹ And for their sakes I sanctify myself, so that they also may be sanctified in truth.

Contemplation

1. What word, phrase, or image from either of the two passages resonates with you?
2. What connection can you make to your own life?
3. What might God be calling you to do?

Reflection

A few years ago, I occasionally went to Salem, our state capital, for meetings of educators from around Oregon. I would jump in my car, check my fuel level, back out of my driveway, and hit the road. In about fifty to sixty minutes I'd be there. It might have been a little stressful if traffic was heavy or the weather was bad. However, for the most part, it was an uneventful trip. Many times, I arrived without remembering anything about the ride.

Traveling in the sixth century was a different matter. The Roman Empire had collapsed in the West, and Europe was being overrun by barbarian tribes. Most likely, the monks traveled on foot and were likely to encounter all manner of people and circumstances. Prayers for their journey were undeniably necessary, and they returned with their heads full of the sights and smells and temptations experienced on their travel adventure. Benedict wanted to preserve the sacred, sanctuary nature of the monastery. Tales of the traveler's experiences would not necessarily be very edifying, especially to the young monks.

Parents certainly know how to censor their conversation around their children, filtering out those bits of information that kids aren't yet prepared to understand or process. Benedict must have had the same concerns around his novices and younger monks. Restraint of speech involves asking yourself, *Is it necessary to say this?* before telling about your various adventures in the world. Would what I have to say benefit or uplift those who are listening?

Prayer

God of great wisdom, guard those who travel. Guide their path and keep them safe. Guard also my lips when I have stories to tell, and give me the wisdom to restrain my tongue. Amen.

10

⌘

CARE FOR OTHERS

RESPONDING TO INDIVIDUAL NEEDS

From the Rule

Let us follow the Scripture, "Distribution was made to each according as anyone had need" (Acts 4:35). By this we do not mean that there should be respecting of persons (which God forbid), but consideration for infirmities. He who needs less should thank God and not be discontented; but he who needs more should be humbled by the thought of his infirmity rather than feeling important on account of the kindness shown him. Thus all the members will be at peace.

Above all, let not the evil of murmuring appear for any reason whatsoever in the least word or sign. If anyone is caught at it, let him be placed under very severe discipline. (Chapter 34)

Acts 4

[32] Now the whole group of those who believed were of one heart and soul, and no one claimed private ownership of any possessions, but everything they owned was held in common. [33] With great power the apostles gave their testimony to the resurrection of the Lord Jesus, and great grace was upon them all. [34] There was not a needy person among them, for as many as owned lands or houses sold them and brought the proceeds of what was sold. [35] They laid it at the apostles' feet, and it was distributed to each as any had need.

Contemplation

1. What word, phrase, or image from either of the two passages resonates with you?
2. What connection can you make to your own life?
3. What might God be calling you to do?

Reflection

I remember being taught the difference between "equality" and "equity." Equality means treating everyone exactly the same and giving the same to all regardless of circumstances. Equity means meeting each person's individual need. Giving two children an equal chance to claim a prize at the top of the stairs isn't fair if one is able-bodied and the other has a physical disability. Giving two men the same meal, when one has just finished a sumptuous feast and the other hasn't eaten for days, doesn't make sense.

Benedict, in this chapter and throughout the Rule, clearly stands on the side of equity rather than equality. And he follows the principle followed by the early church. The principle, however, requires awareness and sensitivity. One does not have to be conscious of needs to give to everyone equally; one only has to be good at division. However, to meet individual needs requires being watchful and sensitive to those who have less. Equity is the practice that requires love.

Prayer

Loving God, help us to be alert to others' needs and serve you by giving to others according to their needs. Amen.

CARING FOR THE SICK

From the Rule

Before all things and above all things, care must be taken of the sick, so that they will be served as if they were Christ in person; for He Himself said, "I was sick, and you visited Me" (Matt. 25:36), and, "What you did for one of these least ones, you did for Me" (Matt. 25:40). But let the sick on their part consider that they are being served for the honor of God, and let them not annoy their sisters who are serving them by their unnecessary demands. Yet they should be patiently borne with, because from such as these is gained a more abundant reward. Therefore, the Abbot shall take the greatest care that they suffer no neglect.

For these sick let there be assigned a special room and an attendant who is God-fearing, diligent, and solicitous. Let the use of baths be afforded the sick as often as may be expedient; but to the healthy, and especially to the young, let them be granted more rarely. Moreover, let the use of meat be granted to the sick who are very weak, for the restoration of their strength; but when they are convalescent, let all abstain from meat as usual.

The Abbot shall take the greatest care that the sick be not neglected by the cellarers or the attendants; for he also is responsible for what is done wrongly by his disciples. (Chapter 36)

Matthew 25

35 "I was hungry and you gave me food, I was thirsty and you gave me something to drink, I was a stranger and you welcomed me, 36 I was naked and you gave me clothing, I was sick and you took care of me, I was in prison and you visited me." 37 Then the righteous will answer him, "Lord, when was it that we saw you hungry and gave you food, or thirsty and gave you something to drink? 38 And when was it that we saw you a stranger and welcomed you, or naked and gave you clothing? 39 And when was it that we saw you sick or in prison and visited you?" 40 And the king will answer them, "Truly I tell you, just as you did it to one of the least of these who are members of my family,[a] you did it to me."

Contemplation

1. What word, phrase, or image from either of the two passages resonates with you?
2. What connection can you make to your own life?
3. What might God be calling you to do?

Reflection

A very expected act of charity, coming from a sense of duty, is to care for those close to us. It is another thing altogether to tend to those who fall outside our circle of family and friends.

The twenty-fifth chapter of Matthew has recently become one of my favorite passages of scripture because of the radical interpretation it takes on a Christian's role in the world. Caring for others, especially "the least of these," is caring for Christ and requires seeing the Christ in others.

In the Middle Ages, Benedictine monasteries were sanctuaries where needy neighbors and weary travelers could find food, shelter, and someone who would attend to their medical needs. Monastery compounds often had a library, a guest house, and a hospital. The monks performed many works of charity: feeding the hungry, healing the sick who were brought to their doors, and distributing medicines. Their motivation, as Benedict points out, was seeing the face of Christ in those they met.

Prayer

Loving Jesus, who touched the leper, gave sight to the blind, and healed the sick, give me your compassion and grace. Help me to see your face in those whom I meet, especially the most needy. Amen.

RIGOR AND COMPASSION

From the Rule

Although human nature itself is drawn to special kindness towards these times of life, that is towards the old and children, still the authority of the Rule should also provide for them. Let their weakness be always taken into account, and let them by no means be held to the rigor of the Rule with regard to food. On the contrary, let a kind consideration be shown to them, and let them eat before the regular hours. (Chapter 37)

Psalm 37

23 Our steps are made firm by the LORD,
    when he delights in our way;
24 though we stumble, we shall not fall headlong,
    for the LORD holds us by the hand.
25 I have been young, and now am old,
    yet I have not seen the righteous forsaken
    or their children begging bread.
26 They are ever giving liberally and lending,
    and their children become a blessing.

Contemplation

1. What word, phrase, or image from either of the two passages resonates with you?
2. What connection can you make to your own life?
3. What might God be calling you to do?

Reflection

The Rule of Benedict sets down sensible rules (at least as life was lived in the sixth century) for living together in a religious community. The appeal of Benedict's Rule has always been in its balance: prayer and physical work, labor and rest, hospitality and restraint of speech, moderation in food and wine. Chapter 37 of the Rule also emphasizes the balance between rules for eating and allowances for those who need an exception, as an act of holy compassion.

Living in a culture that does not always attend to the needs of the most vulnerable among us, this chapter resonates with me. Almost 20 percent of children in the US live in households that experience food insecurity at some point during the year, and many experience the most severe level of need, where food intake is reduced and regular eating patterns are disrupted. Food insecurity is also a critical social issue among older adults that requires immediate attention. Benedict does not bring up the issues of who is deserving or who is not, or what a feeding program would cost. He would say: *Feed them.*

Prayer

Compassionate Guardian, who loves all your children unreservedly, help me to be an instrument of your love, being sensitive to the needs of those around me, even when—and especially when—they are different from me. Amen.

HOSPITALITY

From the Rule

Let all guests who arrive be received like Christ, for He is going to say, "I came as a guest, and you received Me" (Matt. 25:35). And to all let due honor be shown, especially to the domestics of the faith and to pilgrims.

As soon as a guest is announced, therefore, let the Superior or the brethren meet him with all charitable service. And first of all let them pray together, and then exchange the kiss of peace. For the kiss of peace should not be offered until after the prayers have been said, on account of the devil's deceptions. In the salutation of all guests, whether arriving or departing, let all humility be shown. Let the head be bowed or the whole body prostrated on the ground in adoration of Christ, who indeed is received in their persons.

After the guests have been received and taken to prayer, let the Superior or someone appointed by him sit with them. Let the divine law be read before the guest for his edification, and then let all kindness be shown him. The Superior shall break his fast for the sake of a guest, unless it happens to be a principal fast day which may not be violated. The brethren, however, shall observe the customary fasts. Let the Abbot give the guests water for their hands; and let both Abbot and community wash the feet of all guests. After the washing of the feet let them say this verse: "We have received Your mercy, O God, in the midst of Your temple" (Ps. 47[48]:10).

In the reception of the poor and of pilgrims the greatest care and solicitude should be shown, because it is especially in them that Christ is received; for as far as the rich are concerned, the very fear which they inspire wins respect for them. (Chapter 53, Part 1)

Matthew 25

[31] When the Son of Man comes in his glory, and all the angels with him, then he will sit on the throne of his glory. [32] All the nations will be gathered before him, and he will separate people one from another as a shepherd separates the sheep from the goats, [33] and he will put the sheep at his right hand and the goats at the left. [34] Then the king will say to those at his right hand, "Come, you that are blessed by my Father, inherit the kingdom prepared for you from the foundation of the world; [35] for I was hungry and you gave me food, I was thirsty and you gave me something to drink, I was a stranger and you welcomed me. . . ."

[40] And the king will answer them, "Truly I tell you, just as you did it to one of the least of these who are members of my family, you did it to me."

Contemplation

1. What word, phrase, or image from either of the two passages resonates with you?
2. What connection can you make to your own life?
3. What might God be calling you to do?

Reflection

Hospitality is one of the hallmarks of Benedictine spirituality. Benedict quotes from Matthew 25, but he could also have referenced many chapters in the Hebrew Scriptures, such as this passage from Deuteronomy 10: "For the LORD your God is God of gods and Lord of lords . . . who loves the strangers, providing them food and clothing. You shall also love the stranger, for you were strangers in the land of Egypt." (vv. 17–19). The apostle Paul exhorts Roman Christians to "extend hospitality to strangers" (Rom. 12:13). So, hospitality is not only a Benedictine principle, but a biblical principle, in both the Hebrew Scriptures and New Testament.

I think of the times in my life when I have received the incredible kindness of others with whom I've stayed while traveling. Such a gift touches your heart and remains there for many days afterward. I remember my times visiting a favorite monastery where I have been touched by the generous intentions of the monks who have fed me, given me a clean, comfortable room to sleep in, and engaged me in welcoming conversation. I often find myself very emotional when it is time to leave and, on my last visit, became quite choked up while saying my goodbyes. At the root of the hospitality I received was love.

Prayer

Loving God, who cares for the stranger as his own, thank you for the many kindnesses shown me, and keep me mindful of them as I have opportunity to show hospitality to others. Amen.

FEEDING THE GUEST

From the Rule

Let there be a separate kitchen for the Abbot and guests, that the brethren may not be disturbed when guests, who are never lacking in a monastery, arrive at irregular hours. Let two brethren capable of filling the office well be appointed for a year to have charge of this kitchen. Let them be given such help as they need, that they may serve without murmuring. And on the other hand, when they have less to occupy them, let them go out to whatever work is assigned them.

And not only in their case but in all the offices of the monastery let this arrangement be observed, that when help is needed it be supplied, and again when the workers are unoccupied they do whatever they are bidden.

The guest house also shall be assigned to a brother whose soul is possessed by the fear of God. Let there be a sufficient number of beds made up in it; and let the house of God be managed by prudent men and in a prudent manner.

On no account shall anyone who is not so ordered associate or converse with guests. But if he should meet them or see them, let him greet them humbly, as we have said, ask their blessing and pass on, saying that he is not allowed to converse with a guest. (Chapter 53, Part 2)

1 Samuel 9

[22] Then Samuel took Saul and his servant-boy and brought them into the hall, and gave them a place at the head of those who had been invited, of whom there were about thirty. [23] And Samuel said to the cook, "Bring the portion I gave you, the one I asked you to put aside." [24] The cook took up the thigh and what went with it and set them before Saul. Samuel said, "See, what was kept is set before you. Eat; for it is set before you at the appointed time, so that you might eat with the guests."

So Saul ate with Samuel that day. [25] When they came down from the shrine into the town, a bed was spread for Saul on the roof, and he lay down to sleep. [26] Then at the break of dawn Samuel called to Saul upon the roof, "Get up, so that I may send you on your way." Saul got up, and both he and Samuel went out into the street.

Contemplation

1. What word, phrase, or image from either of the two passages resonates with you?
2. What connection can you make to your own life?
3. What might God be calling you to do?

Reflection

In addition to cells for monks, Benedict's monasteries had rooms for the sick and accommodations for traveling guests. As happens today in monasteries around the world, the guest houses were often filled with visitors, being the early Middle Ages' version of a hostel or B and B. Europe's monasteries were famed for their hospitality, seeing it as their Christian duty, and provided a safe place for all people, rich and poor, to shelter for the night. Standards for hospitality go much farther back in our heritage of faith, as illustrated in the example from 1 Samuel of Saul's visit to Samuel.

Not wanting the quiet life and culture of the cloisters to be disrupted by the louder and less reverent behavior of various travelers, Benedict separated the guests from the monks, even to the point of requiring a separate kitchen for the guest house. Two "capable" brothers were assigned to the guest kitchen, and G. A. Simon[1] speculates that the cuisine there would have been consistently better than in the monks' refectory, where all the monks (capable or not) took their turn in the kitchen. As it is today, food was an essential part of hospitality.

Prayer

Gracious God, give me the spirit of love and a desire to offer my best to those who stay in my home. Amen.

GUESTS AT TABLE

From the Rule

Let the Abbot's table always be with the guests and the pilgrims. But when there are no guests, let it be in his power to invite whom he will of the brethren. Yet one or two seniors must always be left with the brethren for the sake of discipline. (Chapter 56)

---

1. Simon, *Commentary for Benedictine Oblates*, 391.

Luke 14

¹² He said also to the one who had invited him, "When you give a luncheon or a dinner, do not invite your friends or your brothers or your relatives or rich neighbors, in case they may invite you in return, and you would be repaid. ¹³ But when you give a banquet, invite the poor, the crippled, the lame, and the blind. ¹⁴ And you will be blessed, because they cannot repay you, for you will be repaid at the resurrection of the righteous." ¹⁵ One of the dinner guests, on hearing this, said to him, "Blessed is anyone who will eat bread in the kingdom of God!"

¹⁶ Then Jesus said to him, "Someone gave a great dinner and invited many. ¹⁷ At the time for the dinner he sent his slave to say to those who had been invited, 'Come; for everything is ready now.' ¹⁸ But they all alike began to make excuses. The first said to him, 'I have bought a piece of land, and I must go out and see it; please accept my regrets.' ¹⁹ Another said, 'I have bought five yoke of oxen, and I am going to try them out; please accept my regrets.' ²⁰ Another said, 'I have just been married, and therefore I cannot come.' ²¹ So the slave returned and reported this to his master. Then the owner of the house became angry and said to his slave, 'Go out at once into the streets and lanes of the town and bring in the poor, the crippled, the blind, and the lame.' ²² And the slave said, 'Sir, what you ordered has been done, and there is still room.' ²³ Then the master said to the slave, 'Go out into the roads and lanes, and compel people to come in, so that my house may be filled. ²⁴ For I tell you, none of those who were invited will taste my dinner.'"

Contemplation

1. What word, phrase, or image from either of the two passages resonates with you?
2. What connection can you make to your own life?
3. What might God be calling you to do?

Reflection

This chapter suggests that, in Benedict's day, the abbot did not always eat with the monks, but in a separate dining room with his invited guests. Philip Lawrence, former abbot of the Monastery of Christ in the Desert, notes that, as it turned out, this system never worked very well.² It was much better for the abbot to eat with

---

2. Philip Lawrence, OSB, "Commentary on Chapter 56: The Abbot's Table," from the website of the Monastery of Christ in the Desert. Accessed July 22, 2019, https://christdesert.org/prayer/rule-of-st-benedict/chapter-56-the-abbots-table/.

the community. However, we can understand the theology behind this chapter. If we are to receive guests as though the guests themselves were Christ, we wouldn't send someone of lower rank to welcome them.

At Christ's table, all are welcome. The Bible is full of references to table welcome. After David sought out Mephibosheth, the crippled son of his dear friend Jonathan, he promised to restore to him the land of his father and grandfather and told him, "you yourself shall eat at my table always" (2 Sam. 9:7). Jesus ate with Pharisees, tax collectors, and scruffy fishermen alike, and food was not the only purpose of this communion. Christ's own loving attention—the gift of himself—was the priceless blessing.

Prayer

Loving Savior, help me to see the Christ in others, especially those around my table. Let my hospitality extend to the giving of myself, attentive to others' needs. Amen.

THE REWARDS OF HOSPITALITY

From the Rule

If a pilgrim monk coming from a distant region wants to live as a guest of the monastery, let him be received for as long a time as he desires, provided he is content with the customs of the place as he finds them and does not disturb the monastery by superfluous demands, but is simply content with what he finds. If, however, he censures or points out anything reasonably and with the humility of charity, let the Abbot consider prudently whether perhaps it was for that very purpose that the Lord sent him.

If afterwards he should want to bind himself to stability, his wish should not be denied him, especially since there has been opportunity during his stay as a guest to discover his character.

But if as a guest he [the pilgrim monk] was found exacting or prone to vice, not only should he be denied membership in the community, but he should even be politely requested to leave, lest others be corrupted by his evil life.

If, however, he has not proved to be the kind who deserves to be put out, he should not only on his own application be received as a member of the community, but he should even be persuaded to stay, that the others may be instructed by his example, and because in every place it is the same Lord who is served, the same King for whom the battle is fought.

Moreover, if the Abbot perceives that he is a worthy man, he may put him in a somewhat higher rank. And not only with regard to a monk but also with regard to those in priestly or clerical orders previously mentioned, the Abbot may establish them in a higher rank than would be theirs by date of entrance if he perceives that their life is deserving.

Let the Abbot take care, however, never to receive a monk from another known monastery as a member of his community without the consent of his Abbot or a letter of recommendation; for it is written, "Do not to another what you would not want done to yourself" (Tob. 4:15). (Chapter 61)

Genesis 18

The LORD appeared to Abraham by the oaks of Mamre, as he sat at the entrance of his tent in the heat of the day. ² He looked up and saw three men standing near him. When he saw them, he ran from the tent entrance to meet them, and bowed down to the ground. ³ He said, "My lord, if I find favor with you, do not pass by your servant. ⁴ Let a little water be brought, and wash your feet, and rest yourselves under the tree. ⁵ Let me bring a little bread, that you may refresh yourselves, and after that you may pass on—since you have come to your servant." So they said, "Do as you have said." ⁶ And Abraham hastened into the tent to Sarah, and said, "Make ready quickly three measures of choice flour, knead it, and make cakes." ⁷ Abraham ran to the herd, and took a calf, tender and good, and gave it to the servant, who hastened to prepare it. ⁸ Then he took curds and milk and the calf that he had prepared, and set it before them; and he stood by them under the tree while they ate.

Contemplation

1. What word, phrase, or image from either of the two passages resonates with you?
2. What connection can you make to your own life?
3. What might God be calling you to do?

Reflection

The striking thing about this chapter of the Rule is the possibility that God sends visitors our way for a special purpose. God may send a visitor to the monastery to give the monks a "reasonable criticism or observation," as three men (angels?) were sent to Abraham to tell him that he and his wife Sarah would have a son. They had difficulty believing the message because of their advanced age but, in fact, it turned out to be true.

This chapter sets a standard for both visitors and their host. First, visitors must not make excessive demands, but simply be content with what they find. Second, the host's welcome should be genuine and generous, willing to receive the guest "for as long a time as he wishes." I find it much easier, as a guest, to honor the first expectation than I do, as a host, to honor the second. (Really? As long a time as he wishes?) Benedict even presents the possibility that the good guest should be extended an invitation to join the community.

The Genesis story of Abraham and his visitors goes even further in describing desert hospitality: washing the guests' feet, bringing them bread and milk, and preparing a special meal. Benedict has more to say about hospitality in chapter 53 of the Rule, where, citing Matthew 25, he reminds us that "all guests who present themselves are to be welcomed as Christ."

Prayer

All-welcoming and all-embracing God, help me to find contentment in the hospitality offered me and generosity in the hospitality I offer to others, seeing Christ in every person who comes to my door. Amen.

GOOD ZEAL VERSUS BAD ZEAL

From the Rule

Just as there is an evil zeal of bitterness which separates from God and leads to hell, so there is a good zeal which separates from vices and leads to God and to life everlasting. This zeal, therefore, the monks should practice with the most fervent love. Thus they should anticipate one another in honor (Rom. 12:10); most patiently endure one another's infirmities, whether of body or of character; vie in paying obedience one to another—no one following what he considers useful for himself, but rather what benefits another; tender the charity of brotherhood chastely; fear God in love; love their Abbot with a sincere and humble charity; prefer nothing whatever to Christ. And may He bring us all together to life everlasting! (Chapter 72)

Romans 12

[9] Let love be genuine; hate what is evil, hold fast to what is good; [10] love one another with mutual affection; outdo one another in showing honor. [11] Do not lag in zeal, be ardent in spirit, serve the Lord. [12] Rejoice in hope, be patient in suffering, persevere in prayer. [13] Contribute to the needs of the saints; extend hospitality to strangers.

¹⁴ Bless those who persecute you; bless and do not curse them. ¹⁵ Rejoice with those who rejoice, weep with those who weep. ¹⁶ Live in harmony with one another; do not be haughty, but associate with the lowly; do not claim to be wiser than you are. ¹⁷ Do not repay anyone evil for evil, but take thought for what is noble in the sight of all. ¹⁸ If it is possible, so far as it depends on you, live peaceably with all. ¹⁹ Beloved, never avenge yourselves, but leave room for the wrath of God; for it is written, "Vengeance is mine, I will repay, says the Lord." ²⁰ No, "if your enemies are hungry, feed them; if they are thirsty, give them something to drink; for by doing this you will heap burning coals on their heads." ²¹ Do not be overcome by evil, but overcome evil with good.

Contemplation

1. What word, phrase, or image from either of the two passages resonates with you?
2. What connection can you make to your own life?
3. What might God be calling you to do?

Reflection

There is zeal and then there is zeal, so it seems. The Bible is full of all kinds of examples. Elijah, in his zeal, killed all the prophets of Baal. Afterward, God spoke to him, asking, "What are you doing here?!," and Elijah answered, "I have been very zealous for the LORD, the God of hosts" (1 Kings 19:9–10). King Saul tried to wipe out the Gibeonites in his zeal for the people of Israel and Judah. In his zeal for the Hebrew law, Paul was a persecutor of the early church (Phil. 3). Terrible atrocities today are a result of religious zeal.

Benedict makes a distinction between good zeal and bad zeal, and he makes clear that the critical factor in good zeal is love. We should be zealous in showing respect, patiently supporting each other, and obedience to the community. In Paul's letter to the Romans, he advocates being zealous in mutual affection, service, and ministry to the poor. Zeal involves hating what is evil and holding fast to that which is good.

I can think of zealous people in my life who, motivated by their faith, are quick to visit the sick, feed those who are hungry, show affection to others, and live in harmony with those who are different from them in beliefs and values. These brothers and sisters should be our teachers. Most importantly, Benedict admonishes us to prefer nothing whatever to Christ, our ultimate example, who brings us all to everlasting life.

Prayer

Loving God, following the example of Jesus, who welcomed the sinner, healed the sick, and befriended the poor, help me to be zealous in following your example, so that others may see Christ's love in me. Amen.

GOING FURTHER

From the Rule

Now we have written this Rule in order that, by its observance in monasteries, we may show that we have attained some degree of virtue and the rudiments of the religious life. But for him who would hasten to the perfection of that life there are the teachings of the holy Fathers, the observance of which leads a man to the height of perfection. For what page or what utterance of the divinely inspired books of the Old and New Testaments is not a most unerring rule for human life? Or what book of the holy Catholic Fathers does not loudly proclaim how we may come by a straight course to our Creator? Then the Conferences and the Institutes and the Lives of the Fathers, as also the Rule of our holy Father Basil—what else are they but tools of virtue for right-living and obedient monks? But for us who are lazy and ill-living and negligent they are a source of shame and confusion.

Whoever you are, therefore, who are hastening to the heavenly homeland, fulfil with the help of Christ this minimum Rule which we have written for beginners; and then at length under God's protection you will attain to the loftier heights of doctrine and virtue which we have mentioned above. (Chapter 73)

Proverbs 1

2 For learning about wisdom and instruction,
   for understanding words of insight,
3 for gaining instruction in wise dealing,
   righteousness, justice, and equity;
4 to teach shrewdness to the simple,
   knowledge and prudence to the young—
5 let the wise also hear and gain in learning,
   and the discerning acquire skill,
6 to understand a proverb and a figure,
   the words of the wise and their riddles.
7 The fear of the LORD is the beginning of knowledge;
   fools despise wisdom and instruction.

Contemplation

1. What word, phrase, or image from either of the two passages resonates with you?
2. What connection can you make to your own life?
3. What might God be calling you to do?

Reflection

Some might wonder what place the Rule of St. Benedict should have in a Christian's devotional life. What relevance should the teachings of a sixth-century monk have to a twenty-first-century faith? Shouldn't scripture be our guidepost as we learn to be followers of Jesus?

Clearly Benedict's authoritative source is scripture. Throughout the Rule, he cites passages from the Bible, especially the Gospels, Psalms, and Epistles. Moreover, in his final chapter he points to Christ and to the "divinely inspired books of the Old and New Testaments" as the unerring rule for life, modestly describing his own Rule as a minimum guideline written for beginners.

Prayer

Loving Christ, Savior and inspiration for our journey, keep us faithful to the path that you have shown us. Kindle the enthusiasm of beginners in our hearts as we pursue the heavenly path and steadfastly work to build the kingdom of God on earth. Amen.